PANDORA

WE MAKE FREEDOM

Beata Lipman is a television journalist in Wales. She went to South Africa as a child, and lived and worked there for 30 years, first as a teacher and then as a journalist with the Congress paper *New Age*, which was banned as undesirable by the Nationalist government. She was active in the struggle for rights and opportunities for all South Africans irrespective of sex, race, colour or creed. She is a feminist.

WE MAKE FREEDOM

Women in South Africa

Beata Lipman

PANDORA PRESS

London and New York

First published in 1984
by Pandora Press
(Routledge & Kegan Paul Ltd.)

11 New Fetter Lane, London EC4P 4EE

Published in the USA by
Routledge and Kegan Paul Inc.
in association with Methuen Inc.
29 West 35th Street, New York NY10001

Photoset in 10 on 11½ Century Schoolbook by
Kelly Typesetting Ltd, Bradford-on-Avon, Wiltshire
and printed in Great Britain by
The Guernsey Press Co. Ltd., Guernsey, C.I.

Library of Congress Cataloging in Publication Data

We make freedom.
1. Women, Black– South Africa – Interviews. 2. Women –
South Africa – Interviews. 3. South Africa – Social
conditions – 1961–   . 4. South Africa – Politics and
government – 1978–   . 5. South Africa – Race relations.
I. Lipman, Beata.
HQ1800.5.W4   1984   305.4'2'0899668   84–1920

British Library CIP data available

ISBN 0–86358–034–3

CONTENTS

FOREWORD

As women in South Africa we endure more difficulties in our daily lives, and suffer greater oppression, than our sisters in most other parts of the world. In addition, if one is black, one has no political rights at all and is discriminated against in law as well as in custom.

Each year on 9 August, the day 20,000 women of all races went to Pretoria to protest against the extension of passes to black women, it is a good time for me to reflect on why women, especially black women, are still being discriminated against. The employers try to blame the women, saying they are not serious workers, that their jobs are easy, require less skill and thus deserve less pay. But the facts are somewhat different: the real reason for discriminating against black women is that it is good business and highly profitable. But that does not mean that we face the world fearfully, and the great variety of women who have talked to Beata Lipman about their lives and their beliefs show qualities of courage and endurance that augur well for change in my country.

Rita Ndzanga

Since these interviews were taped the political and economic position of black women especially has worsened, if that is possible. At the same time the country is aflame with revolt, and for two years there has been an upsurge of feeling and action against apartheid that the government is unable to quell, no matter how many armoured cars and 'Caspirs' and guns it uses against an unarmed people. For the first time it has become clear that the black men and women who are the majority in South Africa will one day take their full place in political decision-making; they will no longer be deterred from that aim, but in achieving it hundreds die and thousands are put in detention every month, there to be beaten and tortured. Women, black and white, Indian or coloured, are in the forefront of the action.

Beata Lipman
July 1 1986

ACKNOWLEDGMENTS

I would like to thank all those friends and colleagues in South Africa and Britain who gave their time and their help so unstintingly in the preparation of this book; and especially Hilda Bernstein, whose lifelong commitment to liberation and the women's movement in South Africa has helped make that cause so strong.

Chapter 1

INTRODUCTION

I left my home, my parents and my work as a journalist in South Africa in 1963 when, finally, the political going got too hot. Even in that flight the old divisions between black and white, the advantages of whiteness, held their usual sway. It was money and education, here, rather than the right to vote or organise, that made the journey to Britain easier; and our skills brought the offer of passports valid for a year, rather than the one-way exit permits usually offered to political émigrés, in the hope that we might still become 'good whites' and return and work within the framework of the system we so abhorred.

But we didn't go back to the land of sunshine. My parents had been chillingly clear: 'If you go to gaol, we won't look after the children.' New issues, fresh responsibilities and other perspectives gradually took the place of a South African being, in spite of all the aches of strangeness, the lack of the comfortable understanding that grows with enmeshment in one society. I began to feel at home in Britain.

Finally, when I did go back, on an assignment called Sport and Apartheid, it was like returning to someone so well loved that intimacy was immediate. There were tiny, irrelevant changes: white and black actually came out of a soccer tunnel together, blacks now served in white department stores. The realities of desperate poverty and hunger, of segregation, political power and the abuse of that power by the most extreme forms of violence against the person, in gaol and out, of fear and intimidation – all was as before. But the struggles for growth and change, for dignity and the right to a decent life – that, too, was as I remembered it in the 1960s. I felt old angers and strong involvement flooding back.

On that occasion, because of our film camera and some

major forthcoming rugby tour by which rugby-mad South Africans hoped to redeem themselves at the international sporting dock, we had formal and official support – an interview with a government minister as well as George Thabe of the then-powerful black football federation, with freedom supporter Dr Nthatho Motlane of Soweto as well as Hitler-quoting Danie Craven of the white rugby world. I'd managed to slip back to my own country unobtrusively once; why not again? There didn't appear to be an airport list with my name on it, in spite of having worked for the Congress paper *New Age* (every time it was banned we produced the paper again, first as the *Clarion*, then the *Guardian*. . .). No one else cared that those were my proud initials at the end of the Nelson Mandela profile in 1962; or remembered the dawn raids on our flat, with their searches for banned material and lists of names. Fortunately, I had been a very ordinary member of the liberation struggle.

So I returned – to Johannesburg, and Cape Town, Mafikeng, Paarl and Lebowa, with a small tape-recorder and background material from the Institute of Race Relations, from small university groups looking for the truths of black lives, and from the painstakingly detailed exposure of inhumane pass laws, which arose from the daily advice sessions run by a committed human rights group, the Black Sash women. I went to record the voices of women especially, because although more of them than anyone else live their lives right at the bottom of the South African dungheap, they are rarely short on courage, dignity, joy and a profound acceptance of themselves at the centre of the family networks which make continuing survival possible. I paid especial attention to old Congress and trade union friends. Some had been in detention during the years, others had lost husbands in gaol; none seemed to me to have lost heart for the struggle – and their personal lives showed a common resilience. (Where it has seemed appropriate, among old friends and new, I have not hesitated to use a pseudonym.)

Why were the small positive changes that were perceptible in the direction of rights and human dignity so irrelevant? That there were no longer any arrests under the Immorality or Mixed Marriages Act, because they had finally been abolished after years of disuse, seemed totally irrelevant when political oppression, brutality and death continued unabated. The state of emergency that existed for many months in main centres has brought death to thousands, with hundreds more, at any one time, detained in gaol without charge – and with overwhelming evidence of systematic torture and interrogation. Since my visit, some of those I interviewed are also now in gaol. The many thousands who went to prison each month for pass offences are no longer doing so, for the moment, because the pass laws have been lifted. But those who come to town in the desperate search for work are still hounded out: the excuse that is used now is that they do not have their own home in the black townships bordering the white urban areas where the work is overwhelmingly to be found. Even those with their own home are hounded if they do not conform exactly to all the provisions of the Blacks (Urbans Areas) Act, that most vicious and powerful mechanism for the physical, geographic control of black people's lives. How could one call this life any better because of a few minor changes on the sporting field, a few more black faces to be found in restaurants and shops? Economic exploitation by skin colour, lack of political wherewithal to do anything about it and general human misery had not altered a jot.

Or so I thought until I went to Bophuthatswana, where there were children and adults rummaging in the rubbish bins and heaps by the Mmabatho Sun City hotel of dubious 'high-life' note . . . further in to the new black state there were not even rubbish piles, only acute hunger. Whatever modest agrarian economy has existed in the past for the vast majority of South Africa's black people, whether as squatters on white farms or in the infertile and overcrowded black areas, even that has been rapidly eroded by the Nationalists' grand, deeply repugnant master plan. For twenty-five years apartheid has been implemented by the supposed development of Zulu, Xhosa, Shangaan, Sotho and other cultural and national entities. The government has set aside and bought extra land (usually the poorest scrub or hilltop land to be found) for the growth of the spurious homelands associated with that cause.

Four million blacks and half a million Asians and those of mixed blood have so far been moved about the chequerboard for the sake of racial tidiness and the blatant lie that is called separate development. Some have been forced to move a second and even a third time to accommodate fresh, arbitrary orders that arise when there's been a conflict on land or mineral values. Men arrive and number homes scheduled for destruction, orders are given or people are tricked with promises of better land, more clinics, new schools. When the time comes bulldozers move in, trucks pick up belongings; people, time and time again, are moved out on to bare veld, always further away from the towns and the farms that they know. More than a million have been evicted from farms, millions more from 'black spots' where they owned a bit of land; and the uprooting of whole tribes, no matter how courageously the fight has been conducted, has been handled by authority with cunning, brutality and skill.

Whatever small chance existed of wresting a livelihood from the land (and women on their own have traditionally been allocated only half the acreage offered a man) has been diminished and then diminished again. The small, neat, bare plots that I saw at Kwagga's A, B and C in Kwandebele, at Tsetse, Rooigrond and the Barolong village of Dithakong in Bophuthatswana mean the end of subsistence agriculture: in its place a landless people are expected to do – nothing.

Frequently, too, the water is not clean. In the rural areas especially, thousands of babies die before they are a year old from enteritis, pneumonia, kwashiorkor (the wasting disease of malnutrition) and marasmus. Their mothers are hungry, the grandmothers wait for death. Throughout the country, one of every two children under 5 is ill – malnourished, starved, listless and suffering from some or all of the diseases arising from an inadequate diet. But at the same time the black population has actually grown, from 13 million in 1960 to 16 million in 1970, to 21 million in 1980. For most life has got worse over these years, not better; the struggle for survival is more difficult, the misery greater.

In Soweto, and Alexandra township on the other side of Johannesburg, kwashiorkor and enteritis has declined after decades of dedicated nursing and teaching; and in the Cape the same is true for coloured people. But in a country as wealthy as South Africa (where in 1980 the gold mines managed to earn an extra and unexpected £4,000 million when gold prices shot up), there is daily death from starvation. At least 50,000 children died from this cause in that same 1980 – 40 per cent of all black deaths under the age of 5. In the Eastern Cape a university study has shown an infant mortality rate of 333 per thousand in one rural area (in Britain the figure is 13). In fact the United States Population Reference Bureau shows South Africa to have the highest infant mortality in the world. Thousands are dying while thousands more live lives of such acute poverty that intelligence as well as physique is affected; it is macabre, here, to hear government ministers talk of improved conditions and the shuffling off of apartheid for separate but 'equal' development.

The droughts of 1983, 1984 and 1985 in Southern Africa – the worst this century – have brought even greater starvation and suffering. It's not only the lack of rain in South Africa: riverflows have also diminished because of an increased demand for water from agriculture and industry, both dominated by white interests.

South Africa is showing a grotesque new version of Malthus and his theory that over-population (in the sense that population outstrips resources) will always be rectified by famine, plague, war or some other 'natural' device. The device the Nationalists use is to try and force millions of people away from the cities and farms where their hunger is seen and known, and where an outcry is possible. Otherwise, why the dismantling of shacks at Nyanga East outside Cape Town when I was there? Why the banning of the international press from the camp sites where police and army sought to break up miserable shelters and disperse families? The next part of the 'natural device' is that they should be sent to the Transkei or the Ciskei, or Bophuthatswana, there quietly to starve.

The policy arises from the economic need for a limited and more skilled labour force in the towns and an even more limited one on white farms, where mechanisation reigns except during the harvesting – at which time the cheapest labour of all, that of black women, is available from an adjacent rural area. It also arises from the fear that those gathered together in large numbers in the cities with no work will become a threat to the regime; scattered amongst the 'homeland' acreage their power to organise is immediately dissipated. In 1960 40 per cent of the black population lived in bantustans; today the figure is 55 per cent.

It is not only in the rural areas that women, with their special and ascribed responsibilities for elderly relatives and dependent children, have a particularly difficult time. Only 20 per cent of all black women are able to find paid employment – and when they are fortunate enough to get it, it often means 'live-in' in a home where their own children are not welcome and they can see their husbands only rarely. Patricia Thuso, a domestic worker in Johannesburg, spoke for thousands of women when she said, 'We work to feed them, but we do not know our children.'

The interviews – with one exception – are with women. There is nothing especially significant about how they were chosen and chance, proximity and my own views were among the determining factors. A few are historical; most are with black women, many of them city dwellers and very aware of themselves and the oppression they meet as black, as female and as worker. Among them are those who struggle for political change, although they certainly do not all walk the same path towards freedom. The feminists among them have strong, forthright personalities that ensure respect among their colleagues of both sexes, and many of them struggle for parity before the law – tribal or urban – in housing, finance and inheritance.

Black women in South Africa live their daily lives within a framework of apparently immutable laws that have said, for hundreds of years, that if you are both black and female you may not aspire, you are not equal and you have no rights. But those who spoke to me so frankly do not accept their status: they are neither passive nor victim. They certainly do not sit with their hands folded listlessly in their laps.

The struggle for political and economic rights for all in South Africa has never been stronger. Since mid-1984 there has been continuous demonstration and political action by many thousands. When meetings are banned, the funerals of those who have been shot by the police – young and old of all colours, and even babies – become the opportunity for great political rallies as well as the dignity of sorrow.

When rents are raised there are rent strikes. Lack of land, water, an arbitrary police presence in black townships – local harassment and deprivation has been met with a new weapon: a boycott of local shops until demands are met. And as ninety percent of the shops are white owned, and whites wield political power, there has been a consequential easing of local difficulties, even, at times, with the police.

At long last black South Africans are saying that they have had enough. Each action provokes a vicious police and army response, but that only swells the numbers on the streets, voting with their feet and their fists for the establishment of full democracy. It is the young men and women at High School, especially, who say they will die for freedom. The shout of Amandla! Ngawethu! rings clear, and many have already died so that there may be power to the people in South Africa.

Chapter 2

URBAN LIFE –
and sometimes half a life

Adeline Pholosi

Miss Pholosi is a 39-year-old clerk in Johannesburg. She lives in Soweto. She has a son of 18 and a daughter of 13, both still at school.

'I was married by lobola to Mr Mohaka in 1960. I grew up in Soweto, so I'm a "Section 10" person – I've a right to be here. They can't make me leave at the moment unless I take a foreign nationality. I'm a Christian and a believer, but I got married by tribal custom because I was afraid about this nationality business: Mr Mohaka is a Sotho – would I have had to leave straight off if I took his nationality? Now my parents were very upset that I did not get married properly, as a Christian should, but to this day we have not done so. It's even more important now than it was in 1960. He's a foreign passport holder, like someone from the Transkei or Bophuthatswana; and I'm still wanting my children to be South Africans. So, if after all these years, if I were to marry him by civil rights as my parents still wish (and he now does, as well) I would have to carry a foreign passport too. That would mean I couldn't have a house; I won't have what I want. I don't like to stay in Lesotho, I like to stay in South Africa.

'We've been married twenty-one years and we've never had a house together . . . in fact I haven't even got a house of my own. I'm on the waiting list, but there's no housing – I'll have to buy instead. I've been on that waiting list since 1971 – me and 33,000 other people! Now I'm collecting my deposit to buy instead. Even so I'm only allowed leasehold . . . huh! I've been saving for that house. But one thing I don't understand: even though it's a 99-year lease the children are not qualifying for that house . . . when I'm dead they're going to take that house and then the children are going to have to buy that house. Whatever I pay off, they will lose it: they will have to start again to buy that house, I'm putting away 50 rand a week because I have to have my house. . . .

'I'm still living at home in my parents' house . . . it's a four-roomed house . . . we are now eighteen people. Mr Mohaka and I have two children, my sister's got four children – she's not married – the other sister she's got four children; she's married and they are on the waiting list for their house. My brother who has divorced – he's got three children and then my mother's children are two, and they've got two children each.

'Some are sleeping in the kitchen – my sister with her four children and my brother's three children are sleeping in the kitchen on the floor. The grown-up boys are sleeping in the dining room with my brother. I'm sleeping in the small bedroom with my sisters and their children; my father in their bedroom with the three children.

'It means I haven't got, really, a life with my husband. He sleeps in the mines – he's a clerk there, but there's no room for us there. If I want to go to see him or I want to make love I must go to him to discuss where we can go and get the room outside the location, next to the mines. We do that after two months or after three months because everybody don't like that at all – the people where we ask for a room. We don't want to go often – it's awkward. Sometimes we want to discuss something and we can't speak because we find we are disturbing the people, and we find we can't talk and discuss this thing – even if we want maybe to shout or something we can't do that – we must go out and talk our secrets outside. He comes to my parents' home to visit once after two months or three months so we can go and ask somewhere to sleep. I also go to the mines . . . I last went to see him when our child was sick – the one who is at school at Lesotho. I went to discuss, but the children of that house where he was were in, for their school holidays, so we couldn't make love . . . we slept separately and he went back to where he's working.

'My whole married life has been like this – we have never stayed together in twenty-one years. If I can buy my house, if he's still working in the mines, because he likes to work in the mines – then at least he can come and visit me once a week or once a fortnight from the mines.

'There's no transport where he's working, just outside Johannesburg the transport is very bad – he starts to work early in the morning at half past four – so he has to live at the mine.

'I like always to be with him – and I can't understand how I can be married to my husband and then I never have the love of my husband. I don't even know what suits him, and he don't know what it is that suits me . . . and I always like to be with him . . . I'm not satisfied – that makes me cry a lot. I don't like to think about that, it upsets me. It would be easy to find love from another man, if I like, but – I have never had a full love to him: when I find him, it's always like a new love every time . . . it would be impossible to leave him and find somebody else.

'The children keep wanting to know – when are they going to have their own home, and when are they going to be together with their father – they miss their father. Children need both parents there, to talk to them, to discipline them, to love them . . . they do, it's very important for children to have their parents next to them. That's the thing that makes me so cross – having no house, my husband not next to me. I don't know our love.'

She has had two holidays with him in all these years, believes his love for her has remained strong in spite of all these difficulties – believes too that he takes a lover now and then but has never taxed him with it because their difficulties are so great. The soft longing of her voice. . . .

Ina Perlman

Ina Perlman, of the South African Institute of Race Relations, went often to Kliptown during the winter of 1981.

'The first day I went out to Kliptown with Cecil Bedwe – OK. I'd been going in and out, but we went out specifically in terms of the West Rand Administration Board and the tents and the shacks and all that. We found in this one plot of ground a group of seven people who had been sleeping out there – this one young couple had been sleeping out there for six weeks. Their home had been demolished, they had put up a shack and that had been demolished as well. There was a mother, father – the mother was six months pregnant – and a fourteen-month old baby. The father was working as a weekly worker at one of the big concerns here and had taken a week off from work to try and desperately find some sort of housing. So he had no pay for that week . . . apparently a lot of his money he's been giving to thugs to prevent their being attacked. They'd had no food since Friday . . . and when we arrived there the baby was scuffling around – it had its head in what looked like a stale ice-cream bin and then at some stage it sicked, and it just spewed up undigested pumpkin, rotten orange – it was the most appalling mess. We rushed off and got some milk for the kid, and to see a child almost scream in agony when it got the milk, and almost gobble it down was appalling.

'But OK, that's one side of it, but in Kliptown, only 12 kilometres from Johannesburg, one day when we were out there one of the journalists called us. We found a mother – her husband had worked for the police. . . . I'm still going into that side of the story . . . he had apparently been murdered on duty. There's obviously some foul-up with the pensions, and this I've got to investigate: she apparently took to selling dagga [cannabis] as her only way of earning a living, and got a ten-year gaol sentence. After five years the child welfare appealed urgently so that she could come out to look after her family. She and her husband had been living in Kliptown certainly for twenty years. The landlord had thrown them out of their house, and for the past eighteen months they had been sleeping on the verandah – a recess, not an enclosed verandah – of a doctor's consulting room. The one daughter has a baby of eighteen months which the social worker confirms has grown up on that verandah and another baby of two weeks. And what staggered me was the fact that a doctor

had, every single day, walked into his consulting rooms, seen
this family there, walked out again – never occurred to him
. . . for God's sake, are we a nation with blinkers on? This
particular family are there perfectly legally – there's just no
housing for them. I would say, judging by the one daughter
and the children, that they were living by a bit of the oldest
profession stuff . . . to survive. People just don't seem to
notice, to care . . . in the African community there is still a
tremendous sharing and caring. But even that is wearing
out. . . . She'd been released eighteen months and nobody'd
given a damn . . . the community health worker had
delivered those two babies knowing they were going back
on the verandah: she said there was nothing she could do.
She'd phoned Child Welfare and because they were African
they came under Soweto, and Soweto, whoever it was,
had said, you know blithely, send them along . . . and of
course nothing had happened. And, you know, this goes
on. . . .

'The seven people who were sleeping out in the open – the
one man only had part of a leg, and was obviously a glue-
sniffer and actually so high that he didn't seem to feel there
was anything wrong with the way he was living, when we
saw him . . . he's been there for three years. There was
another old woman and her husband, who we accommodated
in the tents – the old woman and her children have now been
accommodated in those tents, but it's the total lack of
information that whites have. . . . I believe that this is
because they've deliberately put blinkers on. That is the only
reason for this – otherwise how could the minister get away
with the appalling guff he talks in Parliament? Could he say
that in those resettlement camps in Kwandebele there are
only – only! – 196,000 people? Of whom 6 per cent have work?
Anyone who's driven through that area knows that 196,000
is absurd . . . the authorities there have admitted to us that
last year there were 9,000 children in the first four years of
school in those nine villages – that's the first nine villages,
not the other three that are tucked round the corner. And the
chief minister said to us that there were over a quarter of a
million people in the area – they weren't all in the
resettlement camps.'

In 1981 South Africa's minister for 'co-operation and development', Dr Koornhof, told Parliament that there were now close to 200,000 people in Kwandebele, South Africa's tenth homeland. Just over 2,000 of them could actually find work in the territory – he thought another 35,000 travelled to the Pretoria area every day. That means 95 kilometres there, 95 kilometres back, at least five hours' travelling, many rand from a minimal wage spent on the endless journeys . . . and to come home to the shacks in Kwaggafontain C, one of the many 'resettlement camps'. Many are made from corrugated iron, some of bricks from the red clay soil, tin, asbestos block – they have the makeshift neatness of shanty towns the world over, but not crowded together. Not far apart enough to grow anything, either – rusting farm implements next to many homes show evidence of an earlier occupation, the occupation lost with yet another move of thousands of people to suit the demonic planning of the grand master builders for a neat black and white chequerboard South Africa. Do the Ndebele people want to leave their own small farms, their farm tenancies, the bits and strips of land that have provided some sustenance? 'We had to pay to come here with our things on the lorry, forced to leave our crops . . . but here there's only misery. Our old people have not even had their pensions for the last six months – have we come here to die?'

Nearer to Johannesburg, in Kliptown, the police spent months in the most bitter winter weather of 1981 moving black people out of shacks and rooms where they said they had no right to be because the area was for 'coloured' people only. Many, like Mrs Hlalele, have lived there from childhood.

Ina Perlman has worked for many years with men and women enduring such conditions in their daily lives, in the countryside and the towns. The South African Institute of Race Relations continues its research into different aspects of black life under the most difficult circumstances, producing fact sheets and background material, as well as an annual Survey of Race Relations in South Africa – this in spite of active government harassment and investigation over years.

At the time of the Kliptown removals Ms Perlman was working with members of church groups to provide food and shelter and as part of a combined attack on the West Rand Administration Board to stop its inhuman action. She is an energetic co-ordinator of women's self-help groups.

The Johannesburg urban area, like the land surrounding Springs, Benoni, Kroonstad or any other town in South Africa, has rigid residential demarcations which, to no one's surprise and with some ready advantages for land speculators and property developers, follow yet again ethnic and colour grouping. Blacks may live in white group areas only in a domestic or caretaker capacity, tucked away in the cellar or the roof, or the dingy backs of otherwise smart houses. Those who have established some right of tenure for the time being, like many of the estimated 2 million in Soweto's 103,000 houses, find their ghettos overcrowded, their schools drastically underfunded and transport expensive and often inadequate. On a rising scale houses, street facilities and education for Indians and coloureds become slightly better although education only ever really equals that of whites when it breaks the law by ignoring racial demarcations altogether. Many thousands, too, live in single-sex barracks where they may never, officially, have a visitor in their room.

The pass laws, by which black men and women may be stopped at any hour for the proof that they have the right to exist at all in the urban area, are ruthlessly and systematically implemented, to the extent that on any one day, throughout the country, a thousand arrests are made and 80,000 people – mostly men – are in gaol on pass infringements, usually to be 'endorsed out' of the town on their release.

Black townships are deliberately kept as far from the city as historical circumstance and economic reality allow: planning policies link the notion of riot or insurrection with the creation of buffer zones and townships are designed with broad streets that are wide enough for an armoured truck or tank to turn, without reversing between matchbox houses. Indian, coloured, white, black – 1,460 group areas exist to torment civilisation in South Africa.

Near Johannesburg, in August 1981, the West Rand Administration Board had decided to throw squatters off ground they required for 'development' in a sprawling, dusty village called Kliptown. They also began to force the eviction of black tenants who had roomed for many years with land-lords of a different skin colour. The numbers involved were smaller than at the Cape, where thousands were being arrested in the Nyanga bush at the same time; the issues were somewhat different – racial tidying, racial zoning – and also the elimination of 'black spots' where a few blacks, by a freak of an earlier and slightly more tolerant law, actually had freehold rights. The fanatical imperative of apartheid means that no one may share a house, a shack, even a tent unless they occupy exactly the same rung in the colour ladder: this was what informed these evictions, rather than the resettling of people hundreds of miles away in some even greater rural misery.

But the Kliptown upheavals, some of which are reported here, are just as destructive of people, just as impervious to rights or dignity. A minister of the Witwatersrand Council of Churches, Cecil Begbie, bargaining with authority for an end to the evictions, and some prefab shelters, spoke angrily of an attitude that sees some people not as human but rather like an animal that can be 'thrown out into the open'. Yet many of the squatters actually had the right papers to be in the Johannesburg area; but for many years not a single house was built at Soweto, in an attempt to force workers into hostels and families back to a rural base. Instead, hundreds were more or less permanently living as squatters until the men from the board and the police arrived. Then their lives continued out in the open or in derelict farm buildings, using rusty corrugated iron, cardboard and plastic to shelter against a bitter Transvaal winter. Police action resulted in some health care (why had that authority not stepped in previously?), but little else.

The studies that have been undertaken of the undermining effect of such a combination of poverty, lack of resources and apparent inability to remedy matters report that it is the women, rather than men, who respond with the strength and skill to endure in whatever circumstances they find them-selves. Many of those interviewed are deeply angry and many are strong; all feel that it is worth fighting this government 'at all levels'. Ten years ago, for example, it was official policy to destroy every family home in the black township of Alexandra near Johannesburg and build grim dormitory barracks for single people instead. Today, although many of those hostels exist, so do most of the houses: a result of determined community action and people's desire for a home without light, running water or tarred streets in preference to the bare veld even further from the city centre. Such community struggles may not bring the vote but – like trade union campaigns for better conditions outside the workplace as well as within it – they do achieve change, hope and cohesion.

The law, too, is used by human rights groups to bring test cases to try and establish precedents on the rights of a family to stay together near the towns and cities where a buoyant economy is at its strongest. There have been a number of Supreme Court judgments such as the one where Justice Goldstone criticised the pass laws for attempting to separate husband and wife, saying that Mrs Mafiri Mhlongo had the right to be with her husband in Soweto, where she had lived with him since 1974. But whenever such a judgment is given, it does not necessarily mean that the administrators and bureaucrats of the black administration boards implement the law as it now stands, and government, quick to wriggle out of such attempts through the courts, is already planning another omnibus bill (the Orderly Movement Bill) to stop anyone staying in town who does not have 'approved accommodation'.

While many of the interviews in this section are with those who have long established rights of sojourn in the community, with women who have contributed a great deal in Soweto and to the life of Alexandra township, there are also those who remain only by living furtively in the half light, for ever vulnerable because they have the wrong piece of paper or none at all. There are many in Soweto, and elsewhere, whose itinerant life is like that of the characters in *Sizwe Bansi is Dead*, the play by Athol Fugard in which the pass of a dead man (his life lost in a miserable township puddle because of a few pence in his pocket) gives another the chance to remain in the town. Mrs Hlalele has no papers at all, Miss Pholosi no house, and all suffer in one way or another from the disabilities that truncate apartheid lives. And Adeline Pholosi's fear that even if she does finally save enough to buy her leasehold house, her children will not automatically qualify to take it over, is borne out by a government gazette of December 1978, where the minister retains the 'discretion to determine if certain people are qualified'. If you're politically unacceptable, that clause is saying – like so many others – then we'll make sure you neither have the right to buy nor to stay. The control mechanisms, even where the government trumpets what it calls progress for blacks – as in these leasehold rather than council-owned houses – are myriad.

Josephine Hlalele

Mrs Josephine Hlalele was born in 1937 and has lived in Kliptown, near Johannesburg, as a sub-tenant from 1952 to 1981. She is a Southern Sotho from the Orange Free State. She worked at Langlaagte, Crosby and other suburbs of Johannesburg, but never bothered to register for papers. As a black sub-tenant of landlord Mr Johnson, who is classified as a coloured man, she is being forced to leave her premises in the usual colour 'tidying up' that has now taken place in Kliptown. What is she to do?

She has eight children aged 5 to 20; her husband deserted her years ago. Seven of the children are living on a farm in the Southern Sotho 'homeland' of Qwa Qwa with a black employer who thereby gets free labour, feeds and clothes the children and pays school fees for three of the younger ones. How is Mrs Hlalele to get the necessary papers that will prove that she has been in Johannesburg long enough to avoid the cut-off date for ingress; and that she has worked fairly regularly? The Black Sash established that she is a regular churchgoer; the Catholic church in Kliptown will furnish proof of membership since 1952. She will get a Soweto address, look for work, and painstakingly attempt to contact every employer she has ever worked for to get proof of having worked a minimum of ten years in the last twenty-nine.

Will Mrs Hlalele be able to handle these difficulties and complexities? She has little education but a stubborn determination to stay put in an area where she knows she can earn some money every now and again. It is the Black Sash, like other community organisations, that has helped clarify what needs to be done. After Mrs Hlalele's interview with Sheena Duncan, they are prepared to write letters, make telephone calls and provide legal back-up if necessary. The Black Sash, with its crowded offices filled from early morning onwards with patiently queuing blacks in the centre of Johannesburg, in Cape Town and other towns in South Africa, acts as a lifeline.

Ellen Khuzwayo

Ellen Khuzwayo exemplifies the qualities needed in order to work closely and successfully with others, to reach the goals that inform the work of women in a hundred different types of organisation. It's not only through church groups, which are legion, or in trade unions or women's organisations that the work goes on: many participate in small co-operatives to produce goods – like Ellen Khuzwayo's own Soweto Zomani sisters – and others belong to a *mtshaolo* or *stokvel* where they pool money, meet socially and week by week help one after the other to settle their debts with what has been collected ... in informal credit unions based entirely on mutual trust, which make no attempt to earn interest in the market place.

Ms Khuzwayo has been called the mother of Soweto. She is the only woman on the Committee of 10, those elected to represent the local community during the student rebellion and the imposition of martial law in the winter of 1976. She describes her work among women in the poverty-stricken resettlement areas, as well as the background which she believes forged her own values.

'I'm disturbed by the fact that black women are making a

tremendous contribution in their communities and in this country – and there seems to be a vendetta to stifle this, to blot it out: the men, somewhere, are not playing a fair game. They don't give the black women an opportunity to honestly realise their potential and to recognise that potential when it does come forth. They're doing everything to thwart it, and the government has gone further: it has capitalised, in the legislation of this country, on the traditions and customs which all communities have had. People have gone on, adapting their way of life to the life that is suitable now, for today . . . but the things retarding the progress of the black woman have been highlighted – they will say: "It's custom for you, this lobola [bride price] – you are bought and therefore you are the property of your husband." You cannot take any decisions on anything: either your brothers or your brothers-in-law or some other person other than your husband must even go to the extent of making decisions for you. I've had an experience where I was applying for a passport to go overseas. My husband was already dead at that time and I was told that there must be a male figure in my life who must give consent for me to go overseas. And the only person who would give that consent was my elder son – I felt so humiliated that I had to ask in this way. And this young man looked at me and said, "If only people would realise that this home is where it is, we are where we are, because of you." This is a small example: many others exist on very serious issues.

'I'm 66 – I was born in Thaba Nchu. I had a very strong granny and an enlightened grandfather, who never made a decision without discussing it with her. They were quite wealthy, with a farm and animals – he wouldn't slaughter anything without talking to her about it first – not just a statement but a real discussion. He travelled on an ox-wagon to go to college at Lovedale; he was born in 1880, so there was joint decision-making there well before the Great War. It was a marvellous thing for me to see. . . . I trained as a teacher, but after I was married and had my three children I went back to school to do social work . . . now I've just been a student again, in my sixties, at the University here. . . .

'Look, nobody knows the composition of a human mind, nobody. And everybody regardless of their sex, regardless of the colour of their skin, has a certain amount of pride, self-respect, self-confidence. I think the women in Soweto have those qualities, in spite of the poverty, of the denial of opportunity. The desire to go forward has not been obliterated – the very opposite happens. For too long women have sat down, looked at themselves, maybe accepted certain things as the way of life; but somewhere they've stopped and said: "What is happening? Who am I? Who are we? Where do we come from?" And I think this embodies the "why" women have taken the stand they have taken – they are beginning to realise their potential. They are beginning to realise that they are just as human as their menfolk and just as human as anyone else on earth.

'I don't dispute the possibility that 60 per cent of the families in Soweto are now single-parent: the women have to become father-figures. The divorce rate is becoming very high in the towns for the simple reason that women don't take anything sitting any more: most of the men hide behind custom when it suits them; and they throw it out of the window when they don't need it. Many of the women – especially here in town – will not stand it; unfortunately for the children, it means the divorce rate is very high. But then, these are men who haven't been taking their responsibility of love with their children anyhow.

'The problem is that the children do still see him as father. . . . There were no single parents in the old days – now so many families consist of mothers who have to fend in their own way, and see to it that their families keep above the surface.

'For twelve years – '64 to '76 – I worked with women in the rural areas. I was secretary of the Young Women's Christian Association in the Transvaal; right up from the Vaal River to Louis Trichardt. I worked very much amongst the Tsonga women. . . . I was at a disadvantage because I cannot speak Tsonga. I used Zulu – some of them spoke Zulu and some of them spoke English (some were nurses). I met them when they had just been resettled, one of the endless resettlements of South Africa . . . they make people squatters in the country of their birth. . . .

'I got there in the drought season. *Two of every three*

children were stricken with kwashiorkor. There was gastro-
enteritis . . . it was miserable to see children blown up like
that. I didn't know where to start. . . . I plunged in, talking
nutrition to people who had no food. They were lost, but so
was I at first. This was at a place that this government has
now called Gazankulu. I got there and I said, "Look ladies,
maybe we should start by growing vegetables . . . here are
seeds." We specialised on just two vegetables; if we could
grow spinach and tomatoes, this should do something for us.
They said, "There's no water" – they were drawing water
from a dam a mile to half-a-mile away depending on where
your hut was. This was not clean water and yet they used this
water for drinking too . . . some of the goats, the goats were a
menace to whatever they were going to grow. We had to sit
down and devise a means – we said, "Look, we can get some
bush and use it as a fence." Very few responded at first . . . we
put our seeds in and, strangely enough, the crops came up. It
was like a dream; it was like a miracle during that time. We
started talking about preparation, about eating tomato raw
and preparing the spinach; and then we talked about
powdered milk – the only thing that we could get at that time.
We clubbed together as women and went on bulk buying and
we got milk through these clubs; some of the groups did just
that. They shared the powdered milk, and individual families
bought their own sugar. But if you went to Gazankulu then,
you would find no sugar basin that just had sugar: every
sugar basin had mixture of sugar and powdered milk – they
would force you to take this milk in one way or another.

'Then, after this programme, we looked at the major causes
of the gastro-enteritis; what is it that causes it? One major
cause was exposed faeces. The missionaries of the Swiss
Mission Church: I found a wonderful couple there, the
Schneiders. He was a priest; she had trained as a lawyer but
turned herself into a – marvellous – community worker. She
started helping women to sterilise bottles and she did this
judiciously. She went to every home; she sat down: she said,
"You boil it. This is how you boil it – and then leave it with a
bit of water, and with salt. This is how you cover it. This is
how you wash the linen that covers the dishes of the
children."

'Then the Elim Mission Hospital doctors came and talked about the importance of disposing of anything that can bring about flies; and we got the agricultural demonstator who put up the far-fetched idea of putting up latrines. This was in the early seventies; I've just been back to visit, and now there are latrines everywhere.

'Most of the husbands are away on migrant labour in the cities. The women worked in groups – today we are going to dig your lavatory; tomorrow the next one. They made bricks, they collected stones, they dug the holes themselves. With no money. . . .

'Then I realised there was potential for hand work. One of the women just decided one day: she said, "Ellen Khuzwayo, I'm going to school." I said, "To do what?" She said, "To do weaving. I'll come back and teach them here." When she came back she didn't have the equipment, but she didn't stop. I've never seen somebody so resourceful. She used the burglar-proofing of the huts that were there – she said, "We're going to work with this burglar-proofing; we're going to hinge our wool here and we're going to hinge part of it round your waist." I saw the women working with combs they made out of reeds from the river. The evenness of the comb surprised me; that it could comb and make a perfect article.

'These are the kind of groups that are now growing in Soweto; and each new one helps others get going. The groups are fully co-operative: before you produce anything, you don't earn. You get free tuition, but as soon as you finish an article; it could be on the knitting machine, the sewing machine, weaving, pottery – handwork, patchwork – once you produce something you begin to earn. The council at the top is Zamani Soweto – the Sisters' Council, which does the marketing. We're not earning a great deal this way, but it's a start towards the bread and milk we want for our children . . . it's a beginning.

'I feel very much so that we have been worked into a situation where we have had to look hard at ourselves, and hard at ourselves inside and try and bring up this force that can keep any community going, regardless of all hardships, of all frustrations, of all deliberate manipulation to sort of make your efforts to be fruitless.

'We've just got to go on – even if we feel hopeless. We are determined and maybe this is the thing that makes us to be more determined to go on doing those things that we think are worth doing. I mean, if it were according to legislation we would be feeling that we don't belong to South Africa, we belong to some foreign . . . – people begin to say some of us are stateless, and even this very frightening issue we are facing with determination, because we feel if we give in we shall be lost, and we keep on saying we belong here. We are people of this country, we are South Africans by birth and nobody can deny us this.'

Mavis Thatlane

Mrs Thatlane is a hardworking member of the black community at Alexandra township near Johannesburg. She runs a car to enable her to supervise her two businesses with ease and lives in relative comfort, although, like everyone else in the township, she has no electricity, nor water flowing from a tap in her home (she shares one in the outside yard with three other families). Africans and coloureds have lived in 'Alex' since 1912, holding freehold rights, so that – in spite of filthy, unmade roads with deep stormwater gullies down each side and a bucket sewage system – no one has wanted to leave the township for more distant areas like Meadowlands and Thembisa. During the sixties and seventies, as a result of severe government pressure, the population halved. The 50,000 people who remain have lost their freeholds, and by a combination of law and trickery have had very small sums in compensation.

Alexandra township is 9 miles from the centre of Johannesburg where most people find work, and in 1957 thousands walked 9 miles to work and 9 miles home again for ten weeks because they could not afford an extra penny on the bus fare. They set off at four in the morning and returned home late but they won their case: the united action of the bus boycott and the successful fight of the seventies against demolition had a common thread and today the Alexandra Liaison Committee is still the spearhead of community action.

Mrs Thatlane spoke of not seeing two of her children since 1976:

'In 1976 I had three children in high school in Soweto: two were doing their final year Matric and when everything got disrupted, they just couldn't stay on. The boy was very active – politically active; the girl in a smaller way and certainly not nearly as much as him. We, as parents, got no sleep – the police came at eight, or at ten, at twelve or even at three in the morning: all this just to look for him. Twelve whites and two blacks would come, just looking for one boy.

'They would ransack the house every time, looking for him: they'd look under the bed, even in the fridge. Everyone would be woken – it was terrible. So many children were arrested but mine never were. The boy was being sought, but he was just elusive; then he disappeared completely. We only realised when I was called to the police station to be questioned: they knew that he had gone away – they wanted to know if I had relatives in the protectorates of Zimbabwe or other places. When I said I didn't have any they said that as soon as I heard from him I must come and let them know. As a mother I too was concerned, so I said, "You people, too, if you hear about him, I also would want you to come and let me know."

'Eventually I heard from a friend that they'd gone: it took over six months before we knew where they were. We were relieved that they had gone – if they'd stayed around we might have buried them quite a long time ago . . . so it's best to know they've gone, even though it's also heartbreaking.

'It's heartbreaking to lose your children. Each time you dish up, you find that you're missing two plates on the table. I used to bake their favourite cakes when they first went, as if . . . my son loved banana loaf . . . now I can't bear to do it any more . . . he would normally have had the biggest piece! I'm only hoping that one day, somehow, somewhere, I'll be able to see him.

'We need an open education that is fit for everyone, not just being prepared for the type of life that the blacks are having at the moment. When the kids made their stand, we found afterwards that it was only the name that had changed, not the education at all . . . it was still "bantu" education. It's still an inferior education, definitely. Even the adults, the teachers who are trying to upgrade themselves, they find it very difficult.

'Every time we hope for change our hopes are dashed by the very people who made the promises. They do the opposite of what they said. We had some hope that the new prime minister would give us a better deal, but things have gone back to square one. And of course things are sort of fluctuating: at times you feel things are going your way, but the minute you believe that they have just changed to the worse.

'I think they use the assumption that we're intellectually inferior as a convenient excuse – they are working with us; they see we mean business – people wanting a better kind of life. And if you deny us a proper education then it's easier to keep the idea of inferiority going and it's easier (so they think) to stop us ever getting our rights . . . you can see why the Soweto uprising took place.

'They also use the idea that we are temporary residents in the urban areas to try and control aspiration and development; they must know that we are here to stay!'

Since the taping of this interview Mrs Thatlane has once, briefly, met her son and daughter in a neighbouring territory; one has become an engineer and the other is hoping to be a doctor. They have been helped by international aid funds, have not only survived but will be able to contribute their skills in other parts of Africa. They are two of many hundreds who have fled, rather than sit in gaol, because they have taken a stand for the better life that Mrs Thatlane, too, cares about so much.

Lettie Khuzwayo

Ms Khuzwayo has been a nursing sister at the Alexandra health clinic on the western fringe of Johannesburg for twelve years. The clinic, like similar ones at Soweto and some parts of the rural and urban Cape, has had a profound effect on the health of thousands of babies born in the area each year: as a result of a sustained and careful campaign of health education arranged by the mother-and-baby section – plus immediate attention for the gastro-enteritis and pneumonia that so readily accompany malnutrition – infant mortality has gone down and kwashiorkor is seen more usually only in visitors from rural areas. In the midst of acute poverty, squalor and lack of facilities water is boiled, nappies abound which would satisfy any TV commercial and babies have the shiny faces of good health. The contrast with the immediate environment is as strong as that with the rural areas, where there is overwhelming evidence that one in three babies die from poverty and a lack of health care.

Ms Khuzwayo also spends a lot of time working in the community.

'You know, we used to have freehold rights here. When they wanted to get rid of that, they decided to do it by getting rid of the husbands! The police used to wait at the corners early in the morning, take their pass, and "stamp them out". Then you had to leave Alex and go to Meadowlands. So they used to stamp every man out and tell them, "You go to Meadowlands next day." Then they try to abolish your house and you're moved, just like that. But certainly in all the time I've been here they couldn't abolish us all . . . what they've done now is to buy all the land, so the little right to stay now depends on our passbook, just like everybody.

'My husband was born here and his father had a property. We're fighting now because it's been sold to the administration without our permission. In other words, they took it over at a very low price that we hadn't agreed. We love this place. We both work here, the shops are close, our friends are near. We've got Pick and Pay just round the corner – in

Meadowlands and Diepkloof people have to go miles to the cheaper shops.

'There were freehold rights here for more than a hundred years, given by a Mrs MacMillan, but this government is afraid of that, it gives us the power to stay. The new 99-year leases can't even be passed on to the children. . . .

'We'd like to take over the township ourselves and have our own municipality: the running of the place, the financing, the decisions. The roads aren't made, the gutters are filthy, there's only bucket sewerage. We'd like to have proper toilets and electricity . . . at the moment it's a paraffin lamp and candles, which is very expensive; and not easy when the children are at home alone. When we are away, most of the time I worry in the evening: we often get children with quite severe burns at the clinic.

'It's quite difficult, going out to work with children at home. When they were small they had to wait outside the house after school till I got home. There was one that used to be at school at eight, and knocks off at twelve: from twelve o'clock till I got home at four he just roams around. I used to leave food at the corner because there was no one in the yard, everyone was working. He knew where to pick up his food and eat; then I'd go past at four and get the rest. Now he's bigger I can leave the key with neighbours and he comes back and looks after the younger ones. Now also most of them finish school just an hour before I'm done at the clinic; it's easier.

'We no longer find the police in the streets, with lorries packed with people whose houses are going to be knocked down and abolished . . . that was the scene. Because the clinic is just outside the township, on the Joh'burg side, women used to come and sit here at five o'clock in the morning in those days, so that if the police came they could say they weren't in the township. Imagine, every morning they came! They would run across the street to the clinic and the police would just look at them . . . when you ask them why, they'd say, "Now we're not in a proclaimed area, the police cannot catch us."

'We don't see so much of the police now . . . at that time there was a yard with many illegal people staying: you'd find them too outside at five in the morning, making fires with

paper to keep themselves warm; they were afraid to be in
their shelters in the yard in case the police came. Outside
they had the chance to run! What's happened over the years is
that the administration board has bought properties and
then come in and knocked down some of them. We did fight as
a community, as well as by ourselves . . . it was the liaison
committee that was finally successful with the board, after
the government had a lot of bad publicity about us. One thing
though – that committee is all men and there should be
women there as well. Women are strong: when they want a
thing they stand up and do something!'

Carol Molofe

Carol Molofe works as a cleaner in a Johannesburg hospital
for white patients; she earns 20 rand for a 50-hour week; and
because she has been separated from her husband for four
years she lives in the women's hostel at Alexandra township.

'I share my room with three other women. I'm not living
with my children. It would be very nice to me if I stayed
with our children here . . . we are not allowed that our
children should come and visit for us. If they come they are
supposed to stay outside the gate, and we go there and see
them. So it is very hard for me, when I'm a woman, when the
children come and stay outside the gate although I got a place
to stay.

'I got six children. the older one is 21; the other one is 18;
another one 16. There's one is 10; one 8 and another one ten
months old. What can I do because nobody can give me
something to eat? That's why I have to leave these children
with three months old: so I come back to the job, to work for
them and buy everything for them. To pay school fees. . . .

'So I'm not allowed to find a place, where I can stay with my
children, because I haven't got a husband to find a house for
me. If I haven't got a husband I'm going to stay here forever
for my life.'

There are 4,000 women in the Alexandra hostel, mostly four to a room. Specially concealed riot gates and a small gaol for 'troublemakers' are included . . . because of the huge accommodation crisis for blacks in Johannesburg (and also because there's been a major campaign to stop workers living at the premises where they are employed) the waiting list for the hostel is as long again as the numbers there.

Leah Tutu

Leah Tutu is a co-founder of the South African Domestic Workers' Association, which was formed in Johannesburg in 1981 as a result of major complaints by domestic workers about their conditions of work, poor wages (SADWA is campaigning for a minimum 100 rand a month, but most men and women earn less than half that) and appallingly long hours. Employers in South Africa take for granted the appearance of their domestic employees in the kitchen at seven in the morning, provide one or two hours rest during the day and then expect them to remain on duty until the last plate and cup and saucer has been wiped in the evening. That's regarded as 'normal' in most parts of the country; in the Cape hours may be shorter but more women, who specialise in this work, live out – so then have hours of travelling to and from their own homes, which are in other, less salubrious, 'group areas'. Only 20 per cent of black women have any work at all, and as most of it is in the domestic or agricultural sphere the possibility of any kind of close, strong organisation is very limited. A great deal of the work is regarded as unskilled and easy to replace, which also militates against action by the workers themselves. SADWA plans to expand its work to every major industrial part of South Africa and has already negotiated in thousands of individual cases on behalf of its members. A few employers have agreed to join a pension scheme, which will help their workers at retirement, but the majority of those who work in other people's homes will return to rural poverty, having worked a sixty-hour week as long as they can.

'There isn't an employers' association but we can talk to individual employers – we'd much prefer a counter-organisation to confront. Of course domestic workers are very difficult to organise – they work for individuals – their work conditions depend so much on the good heart of the employer that they vary from very reasonable to very very poor conditions indeed. Reasonable – I would say someone who starts work at half seven in the morning, has a two-hour break during the day, and has already had her breakfast time off – comes back at say six o'clock to help cook the supper; and earns something in the region of 90 rand a month. I think that's good and reasonable for working conditions. But then you get the other end of the stick – someone who starts work at seven o'clock, who is expected to work throughout the day, perhaps with one hour's break and at seven o'clock is still in the kitchen, waiting for the "master" to finish so that she can wash up the dinner dishes and go to her room. And here she may well earn only something in the region of 45 rand.'

There is an enormous dependence, psychological and physical, on the ministrations of the maid. The notion that she should leave work at a reasonable hour in the afternoon and that dishes could be left stacked till the morning is unheard of. Long hours, not helping the maid, insisting that everything be done by her in a particular way, are psychological props to a sense of authority, of control. 'Madams' can make life a small and very particular hell and usually, and quite deliberately, don't develop close relationships even over many long years of service.

'It's got nothing to do with the length of time you've been working for the family. For all I know the one who has reasonable working conditions has been working for that family for three years and the other one may have been with her family for fifteen years, and in that way is much more experienced in domestic work.

'So many women have to almost abandon their own

families to do this work – see the children once a year, the children are brought up by a grandmother – they become migrant workers like the men. They become providers of money.

'They are migrant workers; this exploitation of women in that way is a deliberate act by the government which then of course is followed by individuals in their own home. I mean the government sort of starts it off by making such difficult conditions of contract and saying, "Mrs Tutu, you have permission to be in Johannesburg whilst in the employ of Mrs Cloete." Then of course Mrs Cloete will complete the exploitation that has already been started in that way by giving me unreasonable working hours, but that has nothing to do with the government. The fact that my only right to being in Johannesburg is whilst under the employ of so-and-so – a lot of domestic workers suffer under that – if they stop working for that person they're sent "back" to the rural areas: and their employers say this to them. They say, "If you don't do so-and-so, you'll go and starve back in the Transkei, or Bophuthatswana or what have you." They take pride in using this as a stick against their domestic workers.'

The Domestic Workers' Association has registered more than 1,000 members over ten years.

Ms Tutu's mother was a domestic worker, a township woman who had to leave her family in Krugersdorp: she went early and came late, but the difference was that they did see her, and that she was home at weekends. That was before the time when people became contracted to a particular employer; and she had a little more freedom. Ms Tutu was herself a domestic worker before she began work for SADWA:

'I know the work intimately. I don't think there's anything worse than one grown-up woman being tied to another grown-up woman, to be at the mercy of one other person. We all have our weaknesses and some have more than others. Say I have a horrible temper, and this person knows that she can only stay in Johannesburg and work for her children if she sticks by me, then I can do whatever I like to this person and it's a terrible situation.

'All domestic workers would like to see an end to "live-in" – I don't think any woman in her normal senses wants to be away from the family. Some employers do allow the children to come and stay during holidays, although it's against the law. For instance, if you're around Johannesburg at Christmas time, there are a lot of black children around . . . they come from the rural areas and come and stay with the mother in the backyard room. Of course, that's not the ideal place, but at least they see one another. I can't see it happening – I can't see the end of the living-in domestic worker coming just now or in the near future because of the accommodation problem.

'I would like to see nurseries-cum-hostels for children where they stay in a school with live-in facilities, with plenty of good staff and where the parents could visit – rather than stay far away with a granny in the rural areas; where the money is often late arriving because the post is so bad: so you don't even know how often the children have a meal.

'Nobody is in domestic work for the love of it – a lot of them are in domestic work because there is nothing else they can do – 9 million black women have no work of any sort – you know the standard of education we get . . . for thousands of women there is no choice but to find a solution to earning their daily wage by domestic service. I think they would like to stay home and look after their own children. It's no fun going to scrub someone else's kitchen when you could be scrubbing your own but you have to do it to feed your children.'

Busiswe Tembu

The guests ate and talked about women's rights, sexism and the special problems faced by black women in South Africa: that they are regarded as perpetual minors, always under the control of the nearest male relative and never supposed to stand on their own feet, either in law or in a political frame-work that would enable them to work for legal change.

A stout black woman, whose outer clothing consisted of two ragged overalls of differing colours, one on top of the other, worked noiselessly at the table. She had not been introduced to any of the talkative guests by their hostess, nor did she greet them of her own accord. She served food, extra wine, brought clean plates; the sound of dishes in the sink was to be heard until well after midnight. No one addressed her except for the occasional 'thank you' and her employer, except for a few brief instructions, did not speak to her either.

The white liberal talk went on, concerned, above all and pre-eminently, with the rights of black women. Who was the cipher in the background? The guests, embarrassed as they might be, said nothing; their hostess seemed to find nothing amiss. . . .

Busiswe Tembu is one of the million-plus women in South Africa who find a living, if not dignity, in the long hours of service that are frequently as faceless as they were in this city flat on a winter's evening in 1981. Her right to be in the city is completely dependent on one employer because she has not been there long enough. The passbook with this limited 'right' stamped across its pages has her bare-headed picture to prove who she is; she finds even the bare head an affront to her traditional way of publicly covering her hair.

If she falls out with her employer she will, if she does the legal thing, go back to Hlatikulu, to the sad grandparents who depend on her, and the thin, pot-bellied children who have the tell-tale yellowing hair of malnutrition. Mrs Tembu does not make a fuss and her quiet, closed face is patient. She works in an industry where militant communal organisation is hardly possible. She is represented by the South African Domestic Workers' Association and hopes to achieve some change in her working conditions; but she is also desperately afraid of losing her job and at 55 her chances of getting another, with that pass, are non-existent.

Pretty Ntemba

'I came to Joh'burg from Rustenburg, where my mother worked in the house of some farmers growing oranges. When I was 15 I also got a job as a domestic, but the money was so little that I decided to go to Joh'burg . . . I stayed with my cousin at first – he's a legal – but I couldn't get a pass. So I was arrested and sent back to Rustenburg, and the madam who had given me work had a heavy fine too, for having an illegal in her house. But it was no good in Rustenburg: very little money for the work, so I came back again.

'My life is better now. I'm still staying with my cousin, and I do have some work, four mornings, in a house in Westdene. But the best thing comes in the evenings – I work for a man who pays me 20 rand a night, and I take his friends and look after them for him. I'm earning plenty now . . . it's easy to send money to my mother for my sisters and my brother – they still in school. Of course my mother, she doesn't know the work I'm doing in the night, but she's glad for the money. Even when that's sent, there's still plenty for smart clothes, for food and nice things.

'The thing that worries me a bit is how long I can do this work; I really have to keep myself very nice. What will I do when it finishes? I don't like to be poor again. . . .'

There is a ranking order to prostitution in South Africa that is linked to colour as well as price. 'Posh' black women meet white men in clubs and in flats in white areas of towns, those whose price is lower wait on corners. Near the Johannesburg mine compounds there are usually parked vans that do a regular business deal and miners, returning from a year or two-year contract to a rural home, are seen as fair game by women waiting at some staging post between train and homeward bus. I saw white prostitutes at the Sun City gambling enclave near Rustenburg in Bophuthatswana but on the whole prostitution is marked 'black' on the South African job reservation sheet.

Agnes Letebe

Mrs Letebe has spent her working life in Johannesburg as a domestic 'live-in' worker. She's been with one 'madam' for twenty years but does not expect a pension when she retires; instead, her hopes are pinned on the local chief in Rustenburg – her original home, now within the confines of Bophuthatswana – and the erratic monies available for pension funds.

Mrs Letebe is a dedicated and serene Christian. She spends nearly all her free time, Thursdays and Sundays, in the service of her church. On Thursdays the rituals and prayers involve only women but on Sundays – more significant, as the day for healing – men and women come together, the men in charge. Those who are especially good at prayer become healers: the initiation into this work has given Mrs Letebe her greatest joy. The church to which she belongs, the Dominion Church in Christ, is estimated to have a million members and there are thousands of women like her to whom church membership is central to all life's activity.

'I come from Rustenburg but I've lived in Johannesburg twenty-five years. My parents were Christians and believers and we went to church every Sunday – the Dominion Church to which I still belong. I go to church every Sunday and on Thursday I go to the prayers. . . . I've got a special uniform for that: a blue skirt and a white blouse, a belt – a long belt with a whatsitsname – and a white hat that I'm wearing, with blue on it.

'I'm 52 now and I've been in that church my whole life. We're praying for the people, we are the healers. We pray over the water, and they drink it. We're praying for the people who come to be healed – they all get well, without no pills.

'We've got a lot of branches for the church. On Thursdays, at the prayer meetings, there's only women. On Sundays, we're all together, men and women. Then we wear a special long white dress, a green belt, a white doek on the head. We have been preaching on Thursday, on Sunday the men do it. And it's on a Sunday the sick people come, and we pray for them – it's their special day.

'Petrus Motsule is in charge of the church, he's the leader. We're not under the white people, but we are under the law – some people don't register their churches, but we are under the law in Pretoria.

'We are not to fight the laws in South Africa; we are only to pray, to love each other, see. We are praying to be free, but only in love, not to break the law. If we see black people being moved, say from the towns, we praying to God. When you pray, you can live all right . . . we never fight.

'At Easter time, all the branches come together for a big prayer meeting here in Transvaal; in October we going to Newcastle . . . thousands and thousands – there we going to see who can pray the best. It's like an examination in school, to see who will be the best healers. I'm a healer. . . .

'On Thursday, we don't eat – we're going to pray. On Sunday, we don't eat, we're going to pray. We eat afterwards. My favourite part of the Bible is Johanan where he prays that people must leave the bad things, and go to the water, so that he can baptise them . . . we also baptise in the water. And after he prayed, the holy spirit came and they spoke together in that funny old language. And when Jesus came, they said they would go wherever he went. He said, if you believe, you will eat with me and you will follow me. Jesus had no church – He prayed everywhere, and my church is the same. We do not need a house to pray in. If someone is sick, we will all go to them and pray there.

'I've been in this job twenty years, but I won't always stay in Joh'burg – I'll go to my home. I've got a home at Rustenburg, and I'll go back there. I'll get a pension there from my chief. It's Edward Molokhele under Lucas Mangope, president. Sometimes they get 80 rand every two months now in Bophuthatswana when they're 60. If you're really sick, if you can't walk, you may get it earlier. It comes now from the men paying in something every month, but women don't pay.

'My two daughters grew up in boarding school; one now she's working and the other one she's married. I sometimes go home to visit them, when they was growing up.'

The churches of Zion, to which broadly denominational category the Dominion Church in Christ belongs, are independent and wholly black. They worship indoor and out and use the sea and local rivers for baptism, purification and cleansing rituals which are revivalist in tone. None has so far joined the South African Council of Churches in its determined stand against government apartheid. Thursday afternoon is a traditional 'day off' for domestic workers in the city, especially for women; hence the mid-week prayer meetings that Mrs Letebe spoke of. On another such day a small group of black women were at prayer in the Anglican cathedral in the centre of Johannesburg (St Mary's Cathedral of the Church of the Province of South Africa). They too were dressed in uniform, white jackets and berets, with black skirts, and although there are no Anglican women ministers they conducted their service in a side chapel themselves, with singing, prayer and measured ritual. They seemed very close to their sisters in Christ who wore blue instead of black, but their church has a litany of names – Huddleston, Collins, Tutu – set down among those who care about freedom in South Africa.

Outside, in the cheerful, lively, Thursday afternoon bustle, three young black women also sang, using a tambourine and a plastic accordion for accompaniment. They were not collecting cents for Christ or for freedom, but only for the train fare home to Soweto.

Chapter 3

CROSSROADS AND THE NYANGA BUSH

Since these interviews were taped, the Crossroads camp has finally been demolished. After eight years, the government has succeeded in its aim – the removal of thousands of families, men, women and children, from a small patch of scrub land uncomfortably visible from the highway between the international airport and Cape Town. Thousands are in gaol and tens of thousands are homeless. But squatting, the desperate putting together of two pieces of cardboard and some corrugated iron, continues on the Cape flats because there is work in Cape Town and starvation in the countryside.

> 'We haven't got guns we haven't got nothing we are just going to fight with our talk – that's the only thing. We are not prepared to fly away like chickens.' *Mrs Ntongana*

To the outside world the Crossroads squatter camp near Cape Town, with its cardboard, hessian and plastic shacks, looks almost as impoverished and transitory as the camps set up so hastily (and demolished again and brutally again during repeated police action) by the 2,000 Nyanga people living in the bush during the miserably wet and windy winter of 1981. Both groups had attained their desperate and precarious status on the fringes of the city through a combination of the gross privation and hunger in their original, rural homes which had impelled them to trek to the Cape in spite of every legal obstacle; plus the international publicity that accompanied their struggle to stay in the only place where they knew there was some hope of finding work, some chance of being with partners and husbands; and an opportunity to send modest sums back to a similarly desperate family in the Ciskei or the Transkei.

Since 1975 the emergency camp of Crossroads has survived, even grown. Nine hundred administration-built houses in 'New' Crossroads bear witness to that. After years of battles, of arrests, tear gas, demolition, discussion and negotiation, this community has largely succeeded in its basic aim: let us stay, work here, send our children to school. That success has come because there has been time to gain cohesion and organise: time won partly by legal wrangling that staved off yet more of the demolitions that began in

1978; time to organise women's committees, school committees, vigilante groups and support groups to help find the
rent the Cape Divisional Council insisted on, even for a
cardboard and string shelter, because it sat on their land. It
was the continuing stay of execution, as much as the
publicity, that helped the 35,000 people of Crossroads to
survive, as well as their large numbers. And although it has
only been a partial success story because the administration
is still making distinctions between 'legals' and 'illegals',
between those who can stay and those who must go, Crossroads has overwhelmingly shown that united community
action can achieve important gains.

Those who went to the bush land three years later, in 1981,
right next to the administration office at Nyanga that kept
trying to expel them, were quite as desperate as the earlier
Crossroads people but they were never able to gain the time
needed for the growth of cohesion, of organised resistance
with outside support. Nor did they have the time to grow to
the kind of size that made it difficult to dismantle the earlier
camp, in spite of repeated skirmishes.

The first people settled in mid-July; a few days later the
arrests began. There were 1,500 picked up, 2,000 – men,
women with babies – early morning confusion, dawn raids,
the gale force winds and pelting rain that characterise this
time of year in the Western Cape – and as rough shelters were
knocked down and parents taken away, so too, children were
left abandoned. Those not taken in by local churches or
neighbouring Crossroads inhabitants were found, days later,
still in the bush. One boy, 8-year-old Adam, survived four
weeks on his own.

Member of Parliament Helen Suzman told a group of visit-
ing Americans, who saw a raid and the arrests that followed,
that she thought the government had gone mad – but that the
only alternative for the squatters was 'to go back to the
starvation of the homelands'.

In fact a kind of devilish trickery marked government
action this time. It wasn't so much the usual game of promis-
ing legality if only people would come to the office and
register and have fingerprints taken, then using the information in court to bring a deportation order. Nor was it typical
police brutality, or the decision to round people up and force
them into the bush – there to be arrested at the most

inclement and miserable time of the year. Rather, it seemed that the lessons of Crossroads had been learnt: when fifteen sympathetic attorneys went to Langa and Pollsmoor on July 20 to provide legal aid the courts, unexpectedly, shut at four o'clock. The lawyers left, the courts re-opened and the trials continued, with no representation.

Similarly, the government, this time, did not just put people on a bus or train for the Ciskei – it actually made sure no one got off again at the first stop. Reports emerged of babies left behind – and then of babies deported without parents. One mother walked 150 miles in a five-day ordeal, hitchhiking where she could, before she found her 2-year-old daughter at the Nyanga Holy Cross church back in Cape Town. Mrs Gloria Mgaba had eaten only a loaf of bread during the journey – her ration from the prison when she was ferried to Umtata.

Thousands did not accept their deportation and the trains and buses back to the Cape were as full as those that had taken them away in the first place. The government now set up roadblocks – another new measure – and accused ministers and church organisations of providing the return fare. The human shuttlecock action went on for months: an implacable government defending its skilled labour and 'coloured preference' policy while those without the necessary residential or work qualification kept coming back, desperation opposed to the implacable. A well-publicised study by Dr Jan Lange of the University of Bophuthatswana showed why: those who left the Ciskei to work 'illegally' in Cape Town were likely to treble their income – even if they spent nine months of every year in gaol. Those from the Transkei, given the same conditions, more than doubled theirs.

Dr Lange, when pressed, felt the government's decision to maintain influx control was still understandable . . . with the numbers involved in the official migrant labour system slightly on the decline and the growth of a stable urban labour group with skills rather than mobility, government is now consciously seeking the creation of an urban black élite. That demands an influx control that only those with the most obdurate skills, as well as the ability to live underground for years, can counter. At the same time the new élite will be controlled 'for ever' by the promise of a better life in and near the towns, the government hopes, coupled with the threat of a return to the nearest homeland and incipient starvation for those who don't conform exactly to the political status quo in what has now become a host country.

Over the months the struggle to remain in Cape Town became more difficult and by the end of March 1982 there were only 103 people still squatting in the bush. The few who were still able to earn a living pooled their resources with all the others who were unwaged. There were also fifty-four people fasting in St George's Cathedral, in the centre of Cape Town, in the attempt, finally, to establish their right to remain. One of the women in the cathedral, Mrs Xoliswa Mgweba, affirmed that in nine months her squat was raided and demolished more than fifty times, a record, dubious as it might be, that far outdid those who endured the Crossroads battles. (Although those fasting in the cathedral were not molested by police, in spite of being, quite publicly, in an urban area without permission, 526 people had been arrested the previous year when seeking sanctuary in Nyanga's Holy Cross Church. Even the concept of sanctuary, in South Africa, appears to be mediated by the degree of publicity a particular cause evokes.)

Finally, then, 153 were left still struggling where there had been thousands only a year earlier . . . and yet the very struggle itself, like that at Crossroads, has inspired others to take a stand against unbearable conditions. Elsewhere in South Africa Crossroads has become both symbol and crutch, and so has the Nyanga bush nine-months-long battle against yet another enforcement of physical, economic and doctrinal apartheid.

Nohambile Madolo

'I'm 42 and I got four children – they with my brother in the Transkei. Five years ago I came here to the Cape to look for

my husband when he no longer send money for us. So I
worked on the farms at Paarl because I couldn't find him.
Then I found some work in Cape Town – 6 rand a week, and I
can send some money for my children. But now, because I live
in the bush, they put me in gaol for twenty-eight days: I think
now they'll send me to Transkei . . . I've no papers. What can
we do in Transkei? My children are hungry all the time.'

Mrs Madolo took her youngest child, Sibongile, to Pollsmoor
gaol with her for the four weeks' imprisonment: she had only
just been released when I saw her, one of hundreds of women
with babies on their backs, blankets wrapped around them,
or toddlers by their side – out of gaol and waiting for help and
advice at the Black Sash office at Athlone in Cape Town.

Regina Ntongana

During the late seventies Mrs Regina Ntongana, already
active for many years in community affairs and the struggles
of black squatters in Cape Town to maintain some sort of
stable home for themselves and their families, became promi-
nent on the committee of women who – far more than their
men counter-committee – led the discussions and the day-by-
day activity to prevent the demolition of the Crossroads
camp. She was, for a time, chairwoman and one of the chief
negotiators with government: their work led to wide publicity, inside the country and internationally. Today Mrs
Ntongana still lives in the shack from which she helped lead
that struggle. It has no running water, electricity or sewerage and is surrounded by glutinous mud and large puddles
that turn into ponds during the rainy season, but she has
refused the offer of an official house in New Crossroads
because of a lack of community spirit there, high rents;
and also a dearth of parent participation, as well as some
degree of control in the New Crossroads school. In this interview she speaks of her home background (her mother was
active in early Congress and anti-pass struggles) and the

circumstances that led her back from the Transkei to join her husband in Cape Town.

'I first came to Cape Town in 1959 because the granny I was staying with passed away. When I got here there was a big fight because the women didn't want to carry passes – I was very young and didn't know nothing about strikes – back there we doesn't know about strikes. My mother was one of the Federation women, when I came I found they was always having meetings and talk about this. It was difficult to me because I didn't know about it. . . . I mean I just listened to them and sometimes I went to meetings or I asked my mother, "What's going on, why are you trying to be against the government?": then she was sitting down and trying to explain to me.

'I always saw my father just as strong as her, they were both strong, but he believed that a woman is stronger than a man. He always said, "If a woman say a thing she's not going to change, she's going to do it." At that time, too, it did seem to me that the women were stronger, because there was this big raid by the administration board in Nyanga – the men were beaten up but the women were shouting and swearing at the police: the inspectors did nothing to them; they were marching and singing songs, freedom songs.

'When I got married in 1964 I was staying at Nyanga with my husband's family and there was a rule, a sort of law that if you stayed with people you must be registered that you are a lodger. So we went to the office and they tell me my husband is not qualified to stay because he hasn't worked ten years in one place – he was a labourer at Park Gate, Strand Street, but only for four years. So that means that I have to leave, although I have been born in Cape Town.

'I went to Transkei, to my husband's family; it was so sad and bitter to me that sometimes I just have to cry. But he couldn't do nothing. I couldn't do nothing. He say to me, "If you going to come up they're going to arrest you every time." But later on, when two of the children were dead, I just decide I must come up. I come with two, two were already dead, died in Transkei . . . we were starving in Transkei, I must say it. There wasn't doctors there, they were miles away. When I came to the doctor the child was already passed away. It was really and truly starving, all we had was stamp mealies, no fat, a piece of meat if a cattle die. Sometimes we have to drink dirty water; you just take a white cloth and then have to strain it because it's dirty, the cattle are drinking the same water, there's no other place. My baby was seven months when it died, the other one was two years and four months.

'I decided they can do what they like to me, but I am not prepared to stay any more in Transkei, so I came up with the train. My husband was living in the single men's barracks at Langa, so he took me to his auntie and we lodged there, but it was really very difficult, they arrest us every time. We live like that for three years, and then decide we must go to the bushes, for the people there would help us find a place to stay – a few coloureds were staying there, and they say we can stay with them. That was not Crossroads, but an earlier camp: we built a shack for the family. There were water, but no lavatories, just a hole in the ground, and for rubbish collection we dig another hole. Then after a time it was the administration board that said we must go to the emergency camp at Crossroads, because we was in a coloured area . . . they show us Crossroads, and we came here in February '75. It was called a "site and service" camp – at first they didn't try to make us leave.

'Between '75 and '77 we came to be strong, because we had all these meetings every day; we share our views and our thoughts on each and everything, even before the removals. When we first came we decide to make a meeting of women community members, we must elect a few because when the board came during the day the men are at work, only we women are there. It was up to us to find out who is arrest and who is not arrest; then we decided to go and see the lawyers and that's really how we came to be a community, a women's community at Crossroads.

'It was an elected committee after our outside meetings; we decided we must have some in front to lead, we must know who is going to work – so we elected thirty women . . . at first the men didn't like it, they say we do things too fast for them. Later they decide also they must have a men's committee, to come behind us and see what's going on. But the problem for the men was that they were working, and during the day we was going to all the offices to find out what was going on! So we know more than the men . . . sometimes when we put the agenda to them they start to be jealous and they say why does we always know the things; how does we always know the things? Some of them were really jealous, they stop us to have a meeting . . . later on, when we thought, as women, we must sit down and show how things are happening, really they did accept us.

'I suppose we did win that fight, to stay here in Cape Town, and to stay in Crossroads. But now we don't want to go to the New Crossroads they building, now that the demolition of our camp is no longer in front of us. Even though they are brick houses, with running water, and lavatories and bathrooms – the rents are too high. Some of them doesn't work, some are widows, so they are really afraid of it . . . they wouldn't mind if the government can leave the squatters' camp. It's my feeling too, although I know I did spoke with the government and tried to say we want better conditions. Crossroads is all right except when its raining and it gets muddy; but we have got clinics here, we have each other. We're like the township and we wouldn't mind to stay here.

'We really developed a good system as a community. If there's something wrong, we make an agenda – and first the committee decide what it can do, but it doesn't just finish there: we take it as it is and share it with the general residents. And when we've had a meeting to negotiate we also take it back to all the residents. We call meetings: we've got loudhailers, both men and women using loudhailers. We as women reporting some of the matters, although not for a time because there was a misunderstanding between the men and the women, but now things are coming right. It was funny, really, because it was the women who started the struggle – but for a time it was decided that we should have only one committee, and that it should be men. But now things are all right again because they want the women's group again – they say things doesn't go right like they did when we was doing it.

'My husband – sometimes he likes my actions, I must say it. But then suddenly he change and it makes it look as though I like to be boss. Then we sit down and we talk each one and it helps . . . sometimes he say to me, "You were really good then, that really helped us." He does give support.

'We know that black people in other parts of the country look to us – I'm proud when they do it. What made us to be so strong is the struggle and the hard feeling, we are really struggling hard, and so we thought we must stay together: if only they can stay together they can be strong like us. And our women, if we see something wrong we discuss it, never mind it takes the whole night, we don't care. If we doesn't understand it, we doesn't close that meeting, we sit down and discuss – and we wake up tomorrow morning with better thoughts. We sit together every day if necessary, so it's not to say I'm going to put my views alone, but the other one, and the other one – that makes a community really to be together and strong.

'But it was not only meetings – when we decided and had a vote we would take fast action: going to an office here, telling this one we will not be dumped, saying things to the newspapers. We were planning everything, we went to the lawyers. Then the minister had to make a plan, they could not just pick us up and arrest us because the whole community would be standing there. They would strike at night, and in the morning it would be there in the newspaper. We were fast as anything – we didn't have telephones, but we were fast to call our friends and neighbours, to call help where we need help. Now we would like to help these new people being dumped near us.'

Amelia Nzo

Amelia Nzo was interviewed when she was living in the bush between Nyanga East and Crossroads.

'I'm coming from the Transkei –Txala. I was born 1961, 8th of October. I'm in the hospital as a cleaner and I earn 60 rand a month. It's only four hours but I've also got afternoons up to four o'clock, so I manage.

'The problem is this about a pass and I haven't got a place to stay – they gave me a job even though I didn't have a pass. I'm illegal – I've been living in my boyfriend's quarters. The single quarters by Guguletu – but I wasn't allowed to stay – the police chased us away. They knocked on the doors in the middle of the night – they arrested us; but then I went back to stay in the single quarters because I can't do otherwise – they two in the room and the other man he got a lady there also. But I haven't been there for a year now because I was afraid to go there – then I was with my brother at Langa. I got a baby with my boyfriend, when I was staying in the single quarters. I was in the small room with the baby, my boyfriend and the other two. I worked during the day while he looked after the baby, and he worked at night – a little boy. The baby is now gone because I'm now in the new place near Crossroads – I can't manage to go up and down, up and down with my baby. So my boyfriend has taken the baby to his parents at Butterworth, in Transkei, and I'm in the bush.

'We had a tent, but we got nothing now – they took away the tent. Last night in that terrible storm we had nothing, just blankets. We got terribly wet. I haven't been arrested yet in the bush like the others because when the police come I run away – and the time before I had the baby, so I ran too, but from the cold. And I don't feel well, you know – I got the troubles in my womb, so that place is so cold for me, so I run away.

'I can be so glad if they can give us a place while we are waiting there, at the bushes, but there's no one can give me the piece of paper for that, there's no one can give me that because I've only been here six years. But I must stay here because there's no money there, in the Transkei; there's not enough money for us. I'm working nicely in Cape Town you know. I'll have to stay in the bush . . . there's water there, but no lavatories. To get the bus I have to walk – I must walk up to the bus-stop.'

Amelia Nzo's friend

'I came to Cape Town from Transkei in 1969, when I was a schoolgirl, because when I became older I saw that we are dying of starvation there without work. We didn't keep children, either, because doctors are so expensive; when you've got a child and it becomes sick you don't get a chance to get him to hospital – he dies.

'Most of the other people who came to the Nyanga Bush Camp had been in Cape Town as long as me. Most of them had jobs – even when we were in the open space they went to work and came again to the open space – even the women.

'Before we came to that space I'd been living at the men's barracks at Langa – there were many women there. We'd already been arrested three times: the first time they arrested the men and the wives who haven't got babies and we were left because we have got the babies. On the second time they arrested again the women without babies. Then on the third time they first took all the doors out and they came early in the morning, about six-thirty and they took all the people and the children, even the cats and the dogs in the barracks. So we went to court and then we were first to speak at the court, the women with the babies.

'When we came out, we found out that the gates at the barracks had been shut and there are black inspectors at the gate. When we saw it became dark and we didn't have anywhere to go, we decided to go to the churches to ask them for a place to stay. The one group went to St Cyprian's and the other group to St Francis. It's where we did get a place to stay. Then we stayed at the churches about two months, before coming to the open space near Crossroads. We cared to go next to the people who did struggle before and they will help us. We had a shelter, a carpet shelter and plastic ones.

'On the Friday, Mr Lourens of the Admin Board came and asked us to go to the Langa office and said he was going to legalise us there. He sent trucks and vans to take us. When we were there he asked us our particulars, when we came to Cape Town, and he made files for us and he took our fingerprints and he sent us back again to the open space at Crossroads. Then he came on Friday the next week, and said we must go to the office again to listen to what Dr Koornhof said. When we were there, the chief commissioner said he has got the message from Dr Koornhof – all the women must be sent back to the Transkei. Then he would legalise all the men in Cape Town and get work for them.

'Then we tried to make excuses to the chief commissioner and he didn't listen to us. That's why we were taken to the court: they said we are guilty because we were arrested by the inspectors near Crossroads. It's why we from the beginning said we are not guilty, we were only taken by inspectors. We were taken by Mr Lourens.

'Many people came to join us in the bush – when they heard we were there, many hundreds who also have difficulties came along. Some were people who came after the people of Crossroads had been legalised, so they are staying without having the rights; they came and joined the group.

'The people who ran when others were arrested then also decided to come to court. They marched to Langa and said they wanted to be arrested because the others were inside. But when the policemen saw these people coming inside the court they threw them with tear gas. They started to run and they left the children, and other children were lost.

'Most of them didn't want to be bailed out . . . others were bailed, but many are still in Pollsmoor gaol today. I thought it was bad that we didn't make one decision all together.

'Even from the first week people came to help . . . the white people coming to donate food and blankets, and the clothes. It was on this time that we were sent back to the Transkei – that week the white people were not even allowed to come inside with the food.

'The inspectors came with the police to pull down the shelters. Then there was another meeting with the chief commissioner and our bush committee. They said they would only legalise men and wife who are both working in Cape Town; and the men and women who have jobs. Men with no work would be sent to the Transvaal; so would women with no husband and no work. But the people said that if Dr Koornhof is going to legalise people then he must legalise all the people who are there in that open space. We must be in one group, because nothing can go forward if we split. But now the camp is broken – the police are there; even now they are camping there.'

Annie Silinga

Annie Silinga died recently: she was 72 and already bedridden when this interview was taped. Mrs Silinga was at the forefront of the struggle against passes by the African National Congress in 1956. At the time, no black man could remain in city or town for more than seventy-two hours if he didn't have a pass, but women were still free to move between countryside and town, free to look for work or travel to join husband or family in a new home. Mrs Silinga has refused to take a pass ever since – and as a result, when she turned 60, she was refused a pension.

'I was born in the Transkei, and grew up there. In those days we had cows, sheep – there was no shortage of food. There was no poverty then – we ate a lot, and were very happy! The land was still rich, and there was no overstocking or erosion in those days. When I married, I stayed in the Transkei because my husband worked on the mines in Johannesburg, but in 1937 he came to work in the Cape – at Somerset West – and I joined him because my babies had been dying in the Transkei and we wanted the help of a doctor. In those days there were no papers for women, no passes of any kind, and I was free to go where I pleased. I was also free to stay with him: we moved in to Cape Town, in the centre in District 6, and I had five children. I stayed home to look after the children – during the war they made the first township for blacks, here at Langa, and we moved to this house.

'The life with my husband was very good and secure. Now, when I think of those days, I cry – they were so good that it's painful to look back. He treated me very well – we were living our lives according to tribal custom: a girl didn't do modern things, but as her parents told her. I think that was what made me so strong – knowing exactly where I stood from my parents . . . there were no doubts or worries. Today it's different – you see how it is – you can't force a child to do these things . . . but my children are good: they don't drink, they look after me. . . . Look at this phone; my son put it in for me, because he's far away and now he can phone every day and find out how things are for me.

'In 1956 I was an organiser of the Defiance Campaign for the African National Congress. We went to Parliament with our representations, but we were chased away, so I said, "Let's go to these hotels, trains, white buses and everywhere there is segregation, and break that segregation law!" I was the first woman to enter a white waiting room at the station – we defied the bad laws. I suppose I became interested in these things first of all when we had a residents' association. It was called a vigilance committee, and the councillors used to come and listen to our complaints . . . but they never really managed very much. I used to sit and think, and worry, about what would happen to my children under apartheid if I should die – that gave me the strength to fight.

'Now my children look after me. I should have had a pension ten years ago, but as I have always refused the pass – since 1956 – there is no money for me. Without my children I would now be dead! But they have had to take the passes: how could they have gone to school, or taken their jobs, without them? But they always said to me, "You stay like that; don't take the reference book." They also hate the pass.

'I should like to live in a South Africa where black, white and coloured women can all work and live together without trouble. Even now we must try and stand together.'

Alexandria Luke

Mrs Luke was born in Cape Town in 1951 and except for a short stay in the Transkei has lived in the Cape all her life. As soon as she married the attempt to find a home for herself and her husband began, and they moved from one shack to another.

'I built some of those shacks myself and the council kept demolishing them. I had eight children. Then my husband went back to the bachelor's quarters in Langa and again I tried to join him. The officials were not supposed to help me, but they did give us two rooms. There was a cupboard with my cups, we pushed some beds together, I was cooking there. Was a nice room and we stay there till 1975, although they come nearly every day to arrest me. I escape by windows, one o'clock, two o'clock, three o'clock in the morning. I think, "Oh, I'm so tired, I've had enough now." And then one day, another woman was coming to my place. She was calling my nickname – "Alexo". I say "Yah". "Please give me your van (I used to do the funerals with my van) I want to take my luggage, there's a place at Crossroads."

'I decide to go along; it's going to be my chance to get a place now. But my husband was afraid: "My wife, they are going to shoot us if we go in the bush, they will think we are baboons." But I decide to go anyway and we just collect my things and I go.

'That was in March 1975: suddenly, I'm alone in the bush – I just leave the children with my husband – but I'm not getting arrested, not waking up at one, at twelve, at eleven, going to gaol. This place was full of bushes, trees, big trees then – we even saw snakes at first . . . so I build my house. But now, instead of getting arrested, I'm getting my house demolished. This house that we're in now: this house was built seven times! But still, I say to my children, "Come, come, come, all of my children, we sleep here."

'My husband also came. We just sit in front of the house. Mr Bernard from the office came: "What are you doing here?" I say, "I'm building a house," he say, "I'm going to demolish it." I say, "You are not going to demolish it because this is the seventh time I build this house." He said, "Nonsense, the law is the law." I say, "No, the law is nonsense even to you, because where am I going to sleep?"

'That same day they arrest Father Russell at Crossroads and I go to try and help – when I come back, the house is gone; they even took all the iron material this time. But still we build it again!

'Now, really, our struggle has been successful, but there has been so much pain. And the children got behind with their schooling, you can believe – first all those demolitions and arrests, then they had their own boycott. Pogasi is only Standard 4, and he's 15. We can't say the work is finished, but now they do start to give us permission to work.

'Before, even though I was born here, if I'm not working they try to send me to Transkei. That's a dry country, I'm telling you, my dear, it's a dry country. So no chance – when they try to send us straight to Transkei we just drop down at Bellville or Parow and come straight back. Now nearly everyone at Crossroads has permits and we are still busy to help them. Tomorrow the office start to give another 3,582 permits to people here. This is the fourth time they hand out permits – the third lot were those people are coming from Hout Bay, but the others is all Crossroads. Now 3,582 new permits again. Our aim is permits for ever, because South Africa is for everybody, my dear.

'I think we have been stronger than men in this struggle. Our women's committee holds its meetings in the open – we are using our loudhailers, "Ya, come, come, there's a meeting today." They run all over Crossroads, come to the meeting, nice singing and songs. But the men: I can't understand the way the men are acting, their actions are always in night times, it's a meeting – but in the morning you don't hear what the meeting is for.

'Another thing. If government is standing in front of the men it's easier to shoot him, but if I am standing in front of government and telling them what I need, they make an appointment. Then they have to listen what you say . . . they can't shoot women! A big group of men, they go to hit them, but not with us.

'We have to fill in their survey form – but we all permitted now, even those not born here; and we rejected that survey. First the permits came for twelve months, now there is no date. We are permitted now.'

Helen Suzman

Helen Suzman has been a Member of Parliament since 1953 and was for many years a lonely Progressive Party voice. In the reactionary gloom of a Parliament that wields power, despotic and often quite arbitrary, over the lives of 28 million people – most of whom have no representation whatsoever within it – the Progressives play an energetic role that accords with their name, in spite of adopting a programme of universal suffrage within a unitary South African state only quite recently.

'I was the only Progressive Party member for many years: I'm glad that I now have twenty-six colleagues – they've taken an enormous burden off my shoulders, and at present there are many portfolios I don't touch at all. My special interests remain urban black affairs, which means townships like Soweto, and civil rights. That falls under the "law and order" portfolio, and also under justice – in these days with all the detentions that's a big responsibility. I've also retained prisons, and I visit them as often as I'm able . . . hope to go to Robben Island later this session, and I visit the "politicals" in Pretoria gaol as often as possible.

'The other responsibility is women's rights and discriminatory aspects that especially affect black women – they have a triple dose of discrimination as blacks, as women, and in tribal law.

'I don't think there are going to be negotiations with imprisoned black leaders. I think after the Biko death the government was shaken out of its apathy to some extent and was trying very hard, and managed indeed for about two years to prevent any further deaths in detention. To that purpose they appointed what I call the two watchdogs, who are supposed to be able to pop in and see the detainees at any time – in fact no one else has access to them in that manner – and then report to the minister. And for the rest I'm afraid that Section 6 of the Terrorism Act, which of course is the most drastic of all our security legislation, is not to be really amended in any meaningful way as a result of the recommendations of the commission which reported recently on security legislation and whose terms of reference were to examine the necessity, the fairness and efficacy of South Africa's security legislation.

'I came across three very bad cases last year, which were referred to me by an attorney, of three black women prisoners in Pretoria who had been kept in solitary confinement for very long periods although they were convicted prisoners, convicted of crimes either under the Terrorism Act or Public Violence. One girl, Caesarina, she is a girl, a young girl, I think one of the Soweto aftermath, was sentenced to five years imprisonment, she must be now I suppose 20, perhaps a little older, it's hard to tell: but she'd been in solitary confinement for over two years. She had been very hostile to the prison authorities and was not subject to discipline, would not be subjected to discipline: a very hostile and aggressive young woman whom I actually was able to see eventually, and she's no longer in solitary I'm glad to say. But it took a visit from me, and it took an application to court, which failed, but nevertheless after that they did take her out of solitary. She was a difficult person, there's no doubt about it, she was offensive to the warders and so on, but still the way they were treating her was just ridiculous, I mean apart from the fact that it was inhuman it was obviously not having any desired effect. She was really slightly demented when I saw her. Other than that they are treated, once they are convicted prisoners, they're treated quite normally.

'Well, the squatters are out of the cathedral now and the negotiations are proceeding. Over the next three weeks Koornhof has promised that nobody will be arrested. I gather they are now at another church, the Holy Cross Church in Nyanga in the township itself, so they're out of the cathedral and they've stopped their fast. He's promised to investigate individually the cases of the squatters who were fasting and also to examine the cases of the Nyanga squatters who were in the bush the whole of last year . . . being bussed back and forth between the Transkei and the Western Cape.

'My view is that this is an ongoing problem, it's no good bussing people back to areas where there is no employment, no hope of their earning a livelihood, and it's no good telling the men that they can come in and work for the whole of their working lives as contract workers and see their families three weeks a year. To my mind it's a disgusting system. It's the one we've employed in this country for a very long time; it's still employed extensively on the mines. Possibly there was some rationale for it when the people came from outside the country, from foreign countries, at one stage something like 60 per cent of the labour on the mines was foreign labour, but I think once you employ local labour the whole system really should be based on a family system.

'The squatters: most of them say they have jobs. I don't think they're steady jobs necessarily, I think they pick up work as and when they can, the women do domestic charring or they work as laundry women, or whatever jobs they can get. The men pick up odd jobs on construction sites mainly, there's always a shortage of labour for that sort of work and the people take the chance of employing the illegal workers. They're not so keen to take the chance these days because two years ago, the fine on an employer employing a man who was illegally in the area was increased up to 500 rand for the first offence and not less than 500 rand for the second and subsequent offences. So there is rather more care exercised, but nevertheless these men do manage to pick up some job and a study done by an academic at one of the universities showed that it paid a man to come illegally into the urban area and take a job, and even if he landed up in jail for something like half the year he was still better off financially than if he stayed in the Transkei or the Ciskei where there are no jobs at all.'

Chapter 4

RURAL ATTRITION

In the rural areas of South Africa there are wealthy, rolling farms producing excellent maize crops, sugar cane or wine depending on climate and locality. There are extensive sheep farms and prime cattle ranches. Where there is irrigation there are abundant results from the happy conjunction of sunshine and water; and in the fertile plains of the Eastern Cape and the rolling hills of Natal fruit is cheap and plentiful. But this veritable land of milk and honey is reserved for those with the resources, the right to own the land and the freedom to run their business on the backs of a labour force that is hungry, unorganised and easy to exploit. At Pongola in Natal, for example, black women earn 8 to 15 rand for a week's work – but only in season – and at Pasha in Sekhukune the situation is worse: many report that they are paid only in tomatoes that are surplus to the local farmers' requirements. White farmers normally enjoy a high standard of living; black people living in the rural areas and now the bantustans have had, over the years, less and less of the poorest land to till.

The complex of reasons that has brought this about goes back to times of conquest and more recently to plans for 'betterment' and the creation of quasi-independent black homelands. (Betterment – stock-culling, fencing and planning – has been universally regarded as yet another method of control of a black farming, tribally based economy.) Since the Nationalist accession to parliamentary power in 1948, apartheid has not only been about rigid divisions between black and white in every aspect of their lives: it has increasingly meant that black people, too, must inhabit racially 'pure' districts. It has meant, for example, that Bophuthatswana has been able to oppress those of Sotho origin who were unfortunate enough to be pushed into a Tswana enclave near Thaba Nchu in one resettlement – a vicious mirror-image of white-dominated apartheid in which the Sothos are discriminated against on work permits, residence rights and the language of instruction at school. They are harassed as 'illegal foreigners', arrested, shot at and imprisoned.

In the Ciskei the chief minister, bully boy Lennox Sebe, has arrested and tortured hundreds of trade unionists, members of the militant South African Allied Workers' Union whom he sees as a threat to his despotic power . . . those parts of the country where a spurious independence has been accepted are anti-democratic, like South Africa; they are also rife with corruption, bribery and jobs and concessions for friends and relations. 'I don't even bother to go to the labour office any more because I don't have the money to pay to get work' – this from a man in his late twenties, who has never worked.

But whether puppet state or black reserve, black South Africans who have the misfortune to live in the countryside subsist in extreme poverty; and every fresh policy evolved at the centre leads to ever-greater land hunger, smaller sites, less arable land. A study in Kwazulu that illuminates earlier Zulu expectations sounds like an Arcadian dream: 'Traditional well-being in a rural Zulu family would require a sufficiency of amasi (curdled milk), grains and vegetables in season, a minimum of five huts or rooms per family – one for the grandparents, one for the parents, one for the boys, one for the girls and one used as a kitchen and common family room . . . the 150 families seen in Nqutu are barely subsisting on an average income in cash and kind of 14.87 rand a month. They cannot conceivably express any semblance of social graces or 'ubuntu'. They are underclothed and undernourished; they cannot hope to achieve any meaningful educational standards or indulge in any luxuries even of the smallest kinds, like making a trip into town or purchasing a box of cigarettes or a drink, without seriously impairing their own rudimentary diet of starches.'

Today the earlier family structure is inconceivable. It is the old, the sick, the very young – and the women who look after them all – who remain behind in the country or who are sent there. The fourth and 'final' stage of apartheid sees them as useless appendages who must leave the city for ever, but with no means of survival because they are now landless in the midst of plenty. The family life of the Nqutu study has disappeared as rapidly as the means to sustain it.

So it is the women, pre-eminently, who have to try and make do. Those who are relatively fortunate have husbands who send what they can each month, although they themselves are absentees. Others have elderly relatives whose meagre bi-monthly pension, when it's paid, brings some food into the hut. But many are left to care entirely on their own when a migrant family member – husband, daughter or son – stops sending the vital remittance. Women in the rural areas, subject by tradition to parents, husbands, mothers-in-law and paternal grandparents, have in fact if not yet in custom become the head of the household. They scrape a few rand together by weaving mats and baskets, by doing beadwork or selling fruit. Some try prostitution, others (as I saw in Kwandebele) buy bus season tickets en masse and sell them again to travellers at a price that slightly undercuts the company. Everywhere, they try to help one another in small and practical ways. There are attempts at vegetable growing, often unsuccessful because the soil is poor, the water far away and inadequate; while the drought of the past three years has made conditions immeasurably worse.

When black people are dumped out of sight, crowded together in settlements like Onverwacht or Winterveld or Bothashoek, there is no thought of agricultural potential and development – there is only acute land hunger in a country of vast and fertile acres. The new feudal homelands, which encourage the most reactionary and least democratic aspects of tribal forms and institutions, are a dreadful mockery of such poverty. For example, the government has spent 130 million rand on a new, instant capital for Chief Sebe in the Ciskei and his cabinet, if they outlast his terror tactics, are uniformly housed with marble staircases. He has been well bribed to help central government get 'rid' of 2 million of its citizens, in spite of the fact that two-thirds of them still live and work in the 'white' part of South Africa. As in the other homelands, there's little money for industrial growth and less for investment in agriculture; welfare services would be non-existent without missionary help and life is, increasingly, a daily and quite dreadful struggle to survive.

The white tribe believes it has devised a system to maintain black serfs for ever, readily available to work as needed, but it is exploitation that could be overturned by population growth, by political organisation and by hunger. The rural policies are designed to divide people, one from another, along ever more narrow tribal lines and to make them increasingly vulnerable to police and bureaucratic control. Like everything else about apartheid, it is an attempt to diminish the power and humanity of most of the citizens of South Africa.

Letitia Mogabe

Letitia Mogabe lives in the 'homeland' of Lebowa in the Northern Transvaal with her six children and seven nieces and nephews, whom she has looked after since the death of her sister two years ago. Her husband works in Johannesburg, more than 300 miles away. She and the children are rationed to two buckets of water a day from the nearby church mission.

'We were brought here by my husband Obed. He works in town, in Johannesburg. He only sends me 40 rand because where he works he doesn't get enough money. He works and sends only 40 rand. Then I go to the store. I buy a big bag of mealie meal for 15 rand and I buy three bags of coal. I buy sugar and soap and that's the end of that money. If the children get sick then I go outside to borrow money from neighbours. Here there's no work, we just sit around.

'It's very bad here, nothing grows. It doesn't rain. When you have planted nothing grows. We don't know what to do. I don't like it here but I stay because I don't know where to go. Here there is no food. Even if we die here, there's nothing one can do.

'At times it's very hot. Obed doesn't come very often. He

only comes once a year. Where he lives he cleans and makes tea for the white people; where he sleeps it's at the top of the building.

'When he comes everybody's so happy. The children run to meet him at the bus-stop. Some of them cry and when he asks why they are crying they say it is with joy. They never know when he is coming. We wish that we can just stay with him, if the white people wouldn't refuse me, staying with him for about three months to be able to talk and plan things and discuss everything together.

'The only thing that would also make me happy, perhaps, is if I can manage to sell like other people, at the market. Then it might be better.'

She is quiet, desperate, patient and her worn and lined face does not look like her 36 years. Obed, who has managed to come home twenty times in as many years, says,

'It's twenty years I work for one boss in Johannesburg. He gives me 56 rand a month. I send home 40 rand. Me I get 16 rand . . . sometimes I eat half a brown bread the whole day because the 16 rand – you can't eat the whole month. My children too he can't eat with this 40 rand a month, and I can't buy the clothes for my children.

'If I got the month with a holiday I go home to see my children because my children he can't come to Johannesburg; even the policeman come to catch him – say he got no allowance to stay. Me alone – I must stay alone in the room in Johannesburg.'

Miriam Ntlanaka

Miriam Ntlanaka, who is 75, reached Standard 2 at school but has never been able to find work for a wage. She has no arable land or cattle and all attempts to grow vegetables have failed because 'the land is too dry.' Miriam recently bought a few chickens.

'I must try to make a little money somehow, to help look after my people. My son is sick from the mines and cannot work, and the children are always hungry. All six of us live on my old age pension – that's 40 rand, but not every month. It comes every two months. We often run out of money, then we try to borrow – but others are also so poor, they often cannot help us.

'I came to Lebowa from Doornkop in 1974 . . . at that time I had two cows and three goats. They only gave me 50 rand for them – they really were worth more, but I wasn't allowed to bring them here to the new place, I had to sell. There we also had two long acres for mealies and kaffir beans – with good rain it was ten bags of mealies, so we could save money.

'Now we have this hunger all the time. No one has enough land in this new place here in Lebowa: we must find work outside or starve. So many of the babies die – they do not get enough food. That's the only thing in which I'm lucky: at least the children are a bit older.'

Selina Moesi

Selina Moesi was born on a farm owned by whites, where she lived for many years until the farmer moved away; then the family moved to Lebowa.

'When we lived on the farm we had fields to plough . . . we worked for the farmer and earned 10 rand a month for that. We could hoe our own fields and grow groundnuts and tomatoes. It wasn't an easy life, we were poor, but we could just about manage without going too hungry. Now here we are in the tribal authority, and the agricultural department has made plans: that means we have far less land than we are used to.

'According to the planning system they allocated fields by the amount of money paid to the chief. Actually they tell us the plots are one morgen [land that can be ploughed in one morning] but when you measure they are much smaller. We have to get rid of our cattle and of course our good house – we got no compensation for the house. The new planning system means no cattle are allowed, so I took ours to a relative, but they died there.

'Now there is nothing left. People are starting to die of hunger. I don't think people in the cities know how bad it is out here – we are pushed on to smaller and smaller pieces of land, more and more people come: in God's name, what must we do?'

Selina remembers being called to a meeting once with the local agricultural officers and being told to buy fertiliser. 'It costs more than 7 rand for a bag – starving people can't do that.' She believes things can only get worse.

'Once an area is planned we are no longer allowed to chop wood and live as we wish. So we have to buy coal – that costs 4 rand a week. Everything is so different from the time on the farm: we need cash for everything, but we have no work, so how can we have cash? There we had firewood, we could grow quite a lot, we even had a few cattle. Now we are desperate. Do the government and the chiefs want us to die from this hunger? Can anybody explain this terrible planning department that only makes us poorer and poorer?'

Seroto Moeketsi

Seroto Moeketsi lives with her six children on the neat, sandy plot that was allocated to her and her husband many years ago by the village headman of Dithakong, 6 miles from Mafikeng. She is 33 and has been a widow for three years. The two-roomed house, of clay and corrugated iron, has a red polished floor, white walls, thin cotton curtains at the window and a small battery radio next to the bed set high on bricks in one corner. We sit and talk in the gathering dusk about her empty, anxious life, the worry about work – 6 miles away on the hump-backed paths among the rocky outcrops that make this meandering village, without centre or heart, one long stretch of occasional huts among sparse grass and bushes.

The winter light fades rapidly and Boetie, 12, brings in a candle and carefully, gently, draws the curtain on its piece of string so that we can no longer see the evening star. Dithakong has belonged to the Barolong since anyone can recall; the name, Place of Unity, remembers a welcome given to a group of fleeing Xhosas before the siege of what was then Mafeking rather than the new 'state' of Bophuthatswana's Mafikeng.

Boetie goes out again, this time to stir the porridge in the black pot on the dung fire in the empty yard. 'Why didn't I get a pension from the railway?' Mrs Moeketsi asks. 'He worked there thirty-five years – we got nothing.' Mrs Moeketsi has a bicycle and rides to work four days a week in Mafikeng: it brings in enough for school fees, clothes, and books for the syllabus. 'We're among those with enough to eat because I work – we have porridge, coffee, potatoes, bread dumplings sometimes.' In a corner stands a half-empty paper bag with potatoes; the flickering light shows no other food.

She says, 'I feel really alone. Who can I talk to about my troubles? We no longer speak to each other, as we did. . . .' She is not yet old enough to apply for a pension for herself, but those who do find themselves enmeshed in endless queuing, interminable form-filling and finally, if they are among the favoured, an irregular payment of very small sums that often form the only cash income for the whole family. When Mr Moeketsi began work on the railways, pensions for blacks did not exist and now his widow is fearful of an uncertain life. What will happen if she is ill? There are six children to get through school and even then the possibility of work is remote. She is afraid of real hunger and the drying up of their few present resources. Life stretches endlessly, yet only a day at a time. In the meantime, as we talk, the children stand and do their homework in the candlelight.

Chapter 5

A PIECE OF HISTORY –
women's voices in Lefurutse

'. . . the old and shrivelled, some blind, grandmothers and many in their eighties fled across the hills. They had been milked dry by fines and the confiscation of their cattle. With assaults as their daily bread, men and women are hunted like game. . . .' *A newspaper report at the time of the struggle against passes in Lefurutse, 1956–7*

'We want no part of them – not the covers or the pictures or the pages, not the hide or the hoofs or the horns.' *A newspaper report of the same time*

Until 1952 only black men had been forced to carry the passbook that was both symbol and reality of the oppression, lack of power and attempt at complete control of black lives in South Africa. Then, with one of those brilliant stabs at a doublespeak title that oppressive bureaucracies seem to delight in, Parliament managed to pass the Natives (Abolition of Passes and Co-ordination of Documents) Act. Year by year and place by place, bureaucracy, aided by the local police, began piecemeal to implement passes for women as well, which decided where they, too, could live or work, and what they had to pay for those privileges. It did not take long for the news to spread.

Charles Hooper, an Anglican missionary working in Zeerust, in the Western Transvaal, and in the neighbouring tribal area of Lefurutse, heard many discussions about the document towards the end of 1956.

'Our men – what happens to our men who carry these things? They are fugitives, they go to gaol . . . and they call this thing the Abolition of Passes! It is the Abolition of People! We do not think our men want us to be abolished. They are too much abolished themselves.

'When the men are fined, when they are sent to gaol, we still can care for our children. But what of these babies, when the women must carry these passports to prison?

'Who will care for the crops when we are arrested for pass offences? Oh, why do they want to control us all the time? We are not cockroaches or lice, we are people. . . .'

In March 1957, women in the nearby town of Lichtenburg gathered to go to the commissioner to ask the purpose of the books; they collected near an early queue of men, waiting for a bus to take them to work. The police, called out to 'deal with' the women, baton-charged – and angry men from the bus queue threw stones at the police. In an instant, rifles were out, the order was given to fire and four black men lay dead. Many more were injured . . . yet the government remained adamant that it was just trying to issue a simple identity document that would be beneficial to women as well as men. 'Why,' as one woman asked after the shooting, 'if they are giving us a benefit with these reference books, must it be issued with bullets?'

After Lichtenburg no time was wasted – the special pass unit moved on to Zeerust with its tents, cameras and the small books that cost 3s.6d. Women were forced to queue bare-headed to have their pictures taken (a great insult – no adult woman in the rural areas was ever seen without a head covering outside her own home); by dint of persuasion, threat and cajoling the wives of Native Affairs department employees were the first to come forward. Eventually the ones and twos became a small stream – in Zeerust, at least, more than half of all black women took a pass. But it was the only town to achieve that kind of number. In Dinokana, where the high school was shut 'for ever' after it was boy-cotted in conjunction with a pass boycott, Chief Abram Moiloa was deposed when all he would advise the women was, 'This is not a law of my promulgating – I tell you only what I am bidden to tell you. Consider well how you intend to act.' The uproar after his deposition was accompanied by the burning of the seventy-six passes that had been issued (among more than 4,000 women) and deep anger towards those who had taken them. Arbitrary courts were set up to judge the traitors and the police arrived just in time to prevent some possible executions. At night, for some time afterwards, the huts of those who had co-operated with the law, one or two at a time, mysteriously caught fire . . . there was a feeling that the books had been responsible for a fundamental disruption of tribal life, and when husbands and brothers came back from the cities and their work at weekends, they too became involved in the disruption.

As the arrests began of women in Dinokana, for holding unlawful meetings, for the robbery of reference books, for trespass, for the destruction of the books, so in the other villages of Lefurutse the pass unit tried to do its work. In Gopane, where the chief argued that passes ought to be taken, nearly a third of the women took passes – but Chief Alfred Gopane fled into the hills, away from the resulting hostility. In Lekgophung the women informed their chief – and the unit, when it arrived – that they would not take the book. In Supingstad there was suddenly an urgent need for weeding, replastering and visits to distant parts when the unit arrived – the village was deserted on the appointed day. At Braklaagte and Borakalalo the story was the same. The unit tried a new tack, coming back again and again until a few women here and there were finally persuaded. At Easter time, the police began to move in with new riot cars, automatic weapons and the intention to arrest – those who had burnt passes, those who had 'lost' them . . . gradually, as the arrests grew to hundreds and then to thousands, more women took passes. Hundreds more fled from their homes; village life was so deliberately disrupted by the authorities that no post arrived, no pensions, no urgently needed money from the city wage-earners . . . but still most of the women continued to say 'No'. The riot cars – 'Nylons' or 'Kwelas' – were increasingly used in the middle of the night for going to the homes of women thought to be passless. The women were beaten, bruised and lacerated on stomach, thigh, breasts and buttocks, and then arrested and charged . . . but still government could not get its way. Those small brown reference books were the symbol of men's oppression, their miseries at

work and when travelling. As the summer rose to its height
the corn and maize waiting for reaping was left untouched.
The children waited, empty-handed and often hungry at
home while the women sat in gaol in Zeerust, bruised and
angry and waiting for bail. When it was found, in pennies and
sixpences and shillings sent from the towns, it was never
estreated – and of all the hundreds brought to the magis-
trates' and commissioners' courts, only a tenth were fined. As
the bail monies circulated from one to the next, faint hopes
rose – perhaps it might be possible, after all, to win this battle
by using the courts?

The best example of this was still to come: after the burning
of passes at Gopane, the Mobile Column came to arrest the
two dozen women they thought were responsible. Finding
no one at home, they left messages for everyone to be ready
at a certain time to be taken to the Zeerust court. On the right
day the women converged – but instead of two dozen, the
police sergeant and his two Nylons found more than two
hundred women. He ordered the named women to come
forward: 'Oh, no,' everyone said, 'we are all in agreement, we
all hate the books, we have all burned our passes – arrest us
all.'

The police sergeant, faced with a major loss of face (as well
as the practical impossibility of finding his two dozen in the
crowd), decided to arrest them all. He put through a call to
Zeerust, and two large buses belonging to the Railways
arrived to take the women to town. There the gaol was much
too small, there was no food, and the defence attorney on the
telephone from Johannesburg, Shulamith Muller, kept
insisting on proper procedures: there would be no question
of a court hearing that day. The sergeant decided to send
the women home again – but they refused to walk. It was far,
and dark, and the sergeant must send them back by bus. In
the morning, after a night in the police yard, they got their
buses.

On the day of the trial, the barrister and solicitor arrived
from Johannesburg; the police came from Rustenburg, also
more than a hundred miles away. But the 233 women were

not in court. Police sent out to Gopane to discover the cause of the delay found the women waiting patiently – for transport. In Zeerust, the police and the prosecutor suggested to the barrister, George Bizos, that he should go out and tell the women to come to Court. 'Oh no,' he said. 'The functions of an advocate are clearly defined; but bringing his clients to court is not one of them.'

So buses were sent out again, but the women refused to pay to get on – the buses went back to Zeerust and the barrister went back to Johannesburg. The police sergeant tried to persuade the women to come to court (their numbers had doubled, mysteriously, from two to four hundred) but they agreed only on condition that transport be provided free, and that everyone in the village (were they not all against the passes?) be tried. Eventually, all of them assembled in procession, ready to board the police vehicles. They sang, 'Behold us joyful, the women of Africa. In the presence of our baas: the great one who conquers Lefurutse, with his knobkerrie, and his assegai, and his gun.' Finally explaining they were only women, after all, and very tired, they said it was getting late and they could do no more that day . . . the case, as it had to, collapsed, and the sergeant never found the original twenty-four. But the whole campaign could not be sustained. The pressure took its toll; girls left school early and went off to look for work in the towns, in farm kitchens and on the land: that meant they had to have a pass. Families emigrated to neighbouring Botswana. Community life, disrupted as never before, could provide less support – and also, worst of all, the poverty that had always existed was replaced by very real hunger and great misery. The small brown document, that bringer of 'benefits', helped decimate a struggling pastoral economy that, if not self-sufficient, had at least until then been adequate for survival. And, in spite of the occasionally brilliant defence tactics undertaken by different communities, the end was achieved with gaol sentences and heavy fines . . . six months or £50, six months or £100 for burning a book was the staple diet after Gopane; how many could endure that and still defy?

George Bizos

George Bizos was one of the barristers who regularly
defended those who had been arrested as the struggle against
passes in the Lefurutse area near Zeerust reached its height.
He was briefed by a solicitor in whom the women of Lefurutse
had enormous faith: Shulamith Muller had a large civil
rights practice and worked all hours to try and extend the
limited and circumscribed rights of black people, against
whom the police and bureaucracy used as much intimidation
as law in the attempt to make them accept passes at this time.
In his book *Brief Authority*, Charles Hooper describes how
the women continually asked him to get hold of her: 'The
Father can send our words to our lawyer. She understands
these things. She will stop these wild men.' George Bizos was
also one of those sent to try and stop them:

'I think the fact that for the first time they were being asked
to take passes – they were able to move more freely than their
menfolk; they knew what it meant to carry a pass; and once
this was made compulsory in '55, '56, '57, they reacted very
strongly against it. I don't think they saw it just as an
identity document – I think they saw it for what it really was;
they saw it as a way in which their lives would be more
controlled than they had been until then.

'I was briefed on what started as a preparatory
examination on a charge of incitement to murder: trying to
usurp the authority of the state by holding a court of their
own in which they sentenced to death four of the people who
were co-operating with the authorities. Four tribal leaders;
one of them in particular was an impressive man – Michael
Moiloa, from the royal house of the Bafurutse, in many ways
a dignified man; but who, because of his position, co-operated
with the authorities. This so-called "kangaroo court"
consisted of both men and women, and it was one of the points
made by the state in the case. Part of the case made by the
defence was that it was just a khotla, a sort of gathering of the
tribe . . . the prosecutor pointed out that among the 6,000
present there were many women – and since when did women
take part in the khotla or Parliament?

'The chief had been deposed and taken flight and they had decided to put the collaborators to death. They offered the chieftainship to Boas Moiloa, who said, when offered it, that he was an old man, and he had never seen it offered in a classroom, but always in the presence of the people at the khotla . . . if they wanted him to become chief they had to call all the men together; if they applauded him, then he would assume the position.

'He was eventually banished for his troubles.

'After the khotla of the case dissolved the men went off, about sixty of them, on a Putco bus on the way back to Johannesburg. They were arrested, and the would-be victims of the kangaroo court were rescued by Major Wright. But the women then went around, to practically every woman who had taken a pass, and took it from her and burnt it.

'When the police were sent to arrest twenty-four women, who had apparently burnt their passes, they found 200 women waiting. They demanded a bus to be transported into Zeerust, the gaol was overflowing, and they had to be sent back home again . . . the case never really got started. I went there early in the morning to defend them, expecting to see my – by now – 400-odd clients in Zeerust. There was no one. I met the prosecutor, Mr Tucker, who is now Attorney-General somewhere, and Major Wright and a number of policemen, who told me there was this quarrel as to who was going to pay for the bus. The women had told them that if they wanted them in court they would have to pay for the buses.

'It was suggested to me that I should intervene and go and tell them to come to court. If I remember my words correctly, I said that an advocate's functions were well defined, but bringing his clients to court wasn't one of them.

'Some of the women were very tough, illiterate grandmothers, who were not going to take a pass; they felt offended by it. Also, I think procedurally some mistakes were made – one of the complaints was that they insisted that the women should take the doek off their head for the reference book picture, and in the rural areas it was still seen as very insulting for a woman to be forced to be bare-headed.

'One of the women in another case, her name was Gertrude Mpekwa, she went around collecting all the passes – the state

found it very difficult to prosecute her, because those whose
reference books had been taken away from them, generally
speaking, either refused to give evidence or, having made
statements that their reference books had been taken by
Gertrude Mpekwa or someone else, would come to court and
say, continually, "Che a khietse, morena" – "I don't know,
lord." So the prosecutor would ask, "Who took your reference
book?", and the answer would be, "Che a khietse, morena."
The self-defence mechanism was – no one had burnt their
own reference book, someone else had always burnt it for
them. At that stage they hardly got any convictions at all
because I don't think that anybody really gave evidence . . .
but the authorites assume, in this sort of situation, that there
are a couple of agitators, and that, having caught them, the
others would give evidence, instead of supporting them, and
they would gaol them and that would be the end of the
trouble.

'I don't think the authorities really understood the depth of
feeling against the pass in the women. But after these court
cases came to nothing the police really moved in and occupied
the place; they were not going to rely on prosecutions any
more; they had mobile squads that moved around. People
couldn't move about freely and authority was imposed by the
police. They even went as far as declaring a tribal area a
"police area" – there was no such area then, as there isn't
now, in the country. They said, "We're going to do what we
want here and you keep out of it"; and as a result of the police
action, and also of the action by the chiefs, their councillors
and their new bodyguards, they imposed their authority and
the women either fled or took passes and submitted to the will
of those governing them. The whole campaign lasted for
eighteen months to two years.

'Three or four went to prison on the case of attempted
murder, some were acquitted and some had a £50 fine. There
were no major sentences – the man who had acted as judge,
and the man who had acted as prosecutor, each got, if I
remember correctly, three years' imprisonment. I don't think
any of the women went to prison – they were fined.

'The law can be used as a weapon in political struggle, but I
think its use is limited. It requires manpower, it requires

funds. I think it has helped in a limited sense in a number of instances . . . the passes for women campaign did end with all women carrying passes. I think where lawyers and the law did some good was in the farm labour case – that affected mostly men rather than women. Insisting on proper proof, exposing a lack of respect for legality by those who purport to apply the law, do have, I think, some beneficial effect, but of course they can't solve our fundamental problems.

'The African National Congress was declared an unofficial organisation in those areas. It was the first time this had happened – this was in Lefurutse, in the Dinokana and other areas – they said there could be no meetings except for tribal affairs (a regular khotla), and also that you could hold a religious gathering. I was to defend a man, and he said, well, it had been a religious gathering on a Sunday morning. His defence was that this was a meeting which was exempt from the provisions of the proclamation. I asked him why he said it was a religious gathering and he said, "Well, I read from the Bible." I told him that the further particulars given me by the prosecution were that he had made a speech that the women mustn't take passes; that he had spoken of the oppression of the black people by the whites. Oh no, he said, this had been quite correct, but that it had been a religious gathering. "Tell me, what did you read from the Bible?" I asked. And his answer was "Jeremiah's Lamentations, Chapter V".

"Perhaps you could tell me what this is?" He was the local secretary of the ANC – plus a tremendous sense of humour. He always spoke to me in the third person as a sign of respect . . . and he said to me, "I'm surprised that Mr Bizos doesn't know Jeremiah's Lamentations Chapter V. . . . Oh God, why have you forsaken us, why have you allowed our land to be taken by foreigners? Why have we been rendered to a state where we have to buy our own wood, buy our water." He said he had had to bring the text up to date! He didn't get off, because the state was able to give evidence that he said much more than that, and among other things he sold *New Age* . . . it was difficult to persuade anyone that it was a religious gathering.

I think that from '65 to the early seventies, which from the government's point of view was a quiet period in South

Africa, the latent opposition was kept alive by women. It was a difficult period – most of the politically aware women's husbands were in prison or banished . . . those who could speak certainly spoke out; those who could not speak were substituted by other women, who really spoke out, and in many ways challenged the men with words such as, "If you're not interested in doing anything about liberating our husbands from Robben Island, we may have to take over the leadership."

'I think in the urban areas we are very close to a matriarchal society, with the struggle to keep the family going resting mainly on the women, keeping it together and trying to stop their husbands going off the rails. They complain bitterly about their men . . . but when it comes to politics they don't really want to take over from them; rather it's a question of pushing from behind. . . . I believe they are the more stable of the two partners in contemporary urban life. And I think they're closer to their children without always understanding them.

'We were involved in defending the 159 youngsters who were charged with various crimes in 1976, and for coming into Johannesburg, for marching in from Soweto . . . they'd come along to show, marching in the streets of Johannesburg is OK because you don't get shot – if you march in Soweto you get shot. The mothers would come to us, very apprehensive, and say, "Mr Bizos, my boy is such a good boy, he wasn't really marching; I had sent him to buy apples from the street hawker." They were very concerned about them, hoping they would get off, insisting they come out on bail; and the boy would have made a statement to the police, and to us – a political statement, that we did it, and we did it for this purpose; they were not prepared to be untruthful about the purpose for which they had marched into Johannesburg. The mothers were really very concerned and close to these young people . . . fifteen of them to every father we saw.'

Chapter 6

WOMEN IN THE
TRADE UNIONS

Banning, arrest, detention without trial – these are 'normal' government responses to any action black people in South Africa take to try and improve their living standards or extend their civil and political rights. Their organisation and activity in trade unions, from the early days of the mine-workers' strike in Johannesburg in 1946, has usually met with the same blunt and brutal response. Until 1979 blacks were not even categorised as workers, so that they could never – officially – go on strike. Whites who worked alongside their black colleagues have met similar aggression: a prime example is Neil Aggett, who lost his life in custody in 1982. Helen Joseph, who is interviewed here, was banned virtually for life from the garment workers; yet another is Ray Alexander, the founder of the Food and Canning union for which Aggett worked.

The bannings and arrests, coupled with the neat device of sending home early those on a contract migratory labour system who had proved themselves a nuisance and 'trouble-makers' by daring to go on strike, were relatively effective. As trade union militancy grew, leaders were continually lopped off, activists victimised by being refused work next time round. Major strikes in the Durban area during the early seventies met with the usual response (then, as now, it included the use of police, dogs, tear gas and systematic violence).

But by this time management was no longer always quite as keen on this sort of police and government support. It was beginning to look for skill and stability as well as muscle power; concerned about a poor image abroad (especially if it was a multinational); and not always so averse to dealing with a trade union that represented the men and women in its employ. For the first time, instead of trying to knock black unions out of existence, government set up a commission – and after Wiehahn had reported, in May 1979, black unions could for the first time register like their Indian, white and coloured colleagues. Later, migrant workers, too, won the right to join.

The rapid gains now being made by organised black workers, the daily growth in the numbers belonging to black and mixed unions like the South African Allied Workers' Union and the Commercial, Catering and Allied Workers' Union, as well as to umbrella organisations like the Federation of South African Trade Unions and the Council of Unions of South Africa, are, however, primarily based on hard work, good organisation and political understanding. It is within each particular factory, in the negotiations about union recognition, about hours, pay, overtime or transport subsidies that the initial solidarity and strength has grown.

Liz Abrahams of the Food and Canning Workers' Union gives a vivid example of solidarity between groups – black to coloured, coloured to black. Unions are political as well as economic instruments not only because workers may shout *Amandla*! (*Power*!) at a meeting, or have a picture of Mandela or Biko up in the hall, but because they continually disturb the apartheid-laden status quo of rigid demarcations, pecking orders and rights at work as well as in the wider society.

Black trade union work has also not confined itself to the workplace: the wider rights and economic difficulties in the local community – the question of extra rent or hardship on the buses – continually informs it. Support for specific action by a union, for example during the Fattis and Monis dispute in 1979, and the long-running consumer boycott against the East London factory of Wilson-Rowntree when they sacked 500 workers in 1981, has been wide. Local communities and at times the whole country have begun to support such struggles – it led to unqualified success at Fattis and Monis, as Liz Abrahams recalls.

Not all the trade unionists with whom I spoke believe that white and black should join together in one union. Unions with an open membership, too, do not always get men and women of all groups joining it – the South African Allied Workers' Union has not attracted white members during its rapid growth in East London. At other times, as Liz Abrahams relates, different groups work together in spite of government attempts to enforce divisions at a formal level. Emma Mashinini is persuasive in yet another direction – that black and white actually need separate, although parallel, organisation. It is a sign of the richness of the proliferation now taking place that both arguments are put, that so many different approaches meet, today, with such frequent success. More than half the ninety strikes in FOSATU-organised factories were successful in 1981, and companies like Ford in Port Elizabeth and Volkswagen in Uitenhage nearby have discovered that mass dismissal is no longer open to them, in spite of unemployment rates of up to 50 per cent in each area – 'We would eventually have had to hire our own people back,' a company manager said of the skilled people in his employ.

On the Witwatersrand women are especially active in the catering, distributive and garment industries. In the Western Cape thousands work in food and fisheries; evidence everywhere shows that women organisers readily earn the respect and confidence of men colleagues and members – remarkable in a society noted for its sexism, and where many blacks accept historical and tribal attitudes and customs of male dominance without much questioning.

Maternity benefits are payable to women covered by the Factories Act, but the money is always at least three months late instead of helping at the critical time when work is impossible. Most women workers go back as soon as possible, for fear of losing the job – and because they still, too frequently, lose seniority. They are also clearly – often grossly – discriminated against in terms of the concept of equal pay for equal work in spite of recent legislation outlawing such discrimination. This isn't only a matter of differences between white and black, coloured and Indian – the usual South African pecking order ensuring, whether you're a teacher, a sugar-cane worker or a domestic, that you're paid as much according to the colour of your skin as any parity of training – but here very much whether you're a man or woman.

White farmers, as increased mechanisation has affected agriculture, have dismissed most of their black tenant farmers, kept on a few men for more skilled work – and, on a casual, seasonal basis, now hire women to come and pick, hoe or plant. There are well documented reports from many areas where pay for this type of work, to women, is only in kind (tomatoes, more tomatoes, but nothing else, for example), but men, where still employed, receive cash as well as crops. Women in industry earn less than men – black or white. Discrimination in teaching often forces women to resign if they marry, whether black or white. But everywhere, as ever in South Africa, black women struggle right at the bottom of every pay scale; they work the longest hours and endure the greatest misery. In that context it is not surprising that they make such excellent trade union organisers – yet thousands of women, especially those in agriculture and domestic work (which is where most find a place – the figure runs to 2 million) are not organised into any trade union at all. The South African Domestic Workers' Employment Project is the nearest to a union that exists for 'domestics', and those who pick up what they can on an occasional basis on white or black farms have no form of organisation at all.

There is a final point to make about those who are fortunate enough to have work, and well enough organised to be in a useful trade union: if they are seen to become too much in control of their own destiny, there are two further embargoes that may be undertaken against them . . . their permission to remain in an urban area (where most factories are placed) can be revoked because no black, no matter which piece of paper she or he may possess under the urban areas legislation, will ever be a citizen there with rights to stay; and the union could, still, in spite of growth and 'progress', be banned. That is, if police raids, arrests, beating up and the more usual forms of political interrogation have still not had the desired effect.

Rita Ndzanga

Rita Ndzanga was secretary of the Toy Workers' Union and an active leader of the South African Railways and Harbour Workers' Union alongside her husband, Lawrence. She was banned from trade union activity in 1964. In 1969 she was charged under the Terrorism Act, acquitted and then re-arrested. Her husband was arrested at the same time, and their four young children were cared for by friends. She has recently been detained for six months.

'My first interrogation took place on May 16, I was taken to a room at the back of Compol Buildings. Major Swanepoel called me by my name. I kept quiet and did not reply. Other security police continued to question me. Day and night is the same in this room because of the thick, heavy planks covering the windows. I remained standing. It was late at night. One policeman came round the table towards me and struck me. I fell to the floor. He said, "Staan op!", and kicked me while I lay on the floor.'

They poured water on her face. A new team of interrogators came in and told her she would be kept standing until she spoke. During their period of interrogation they began hitting her, then made her take off her shoes and stand on bricks. One of the security police climbed a chair and pulled her by her hair, dropping her on the bricks. They did this again and again each time she fell. 'The man who pulled me by the hair had his hands full of it.'

In 1976 Rita and Lawrence Ndzanga were again detained; he died during interrogation and she was released – the day after the funeral.

'I'm now the organising secretary and treasurer of the General and Allied Workers' Union. I grew up and went to school in Sophiatown when Father Huddleston was here. We grew up knowing that whites were privileged people; as far as we were concerned, we had none. But we were prepared to learn . . . my family weren't interested in politics: it's a family of chiefs. My father made all the rules in the house: he was the boss and his word was always final. My mother never argued; whatever he said she'd say to me, "Your father says this, and you must do it." But when I got married in 1956, there was a very good understanding with my husband, because he was political – and so was I, by that time. We would discuss problems, and approach things together . . . supposing we wanted to buy furniture for the house: we'd talk about it and then go to the shop together to agree on what we wanted.

'I think that our equal partnership in marriage had a great deal to do with our political awareness; that had changed our perspective on a great many things, including personal relationships.

'I'd been married in community of property. When my husband died in detention I then had to fight the legal battle to actually take charge of our joint affars – there was still the attempt to put me in the charge of his oldest male relative. But of course I wasn't having any of that! I went to an attorney, and when he wrote to the administration office they ceased opposing me.

'They transferred our house in Soweto into my name, and I became the legal tenant . . . but I had had the money, and the sense, if you like, to get help from the law. . . . I know widows who have been thrown out. I kept all our goods, too – the only problem was the bank: they wanted to take our money to the bantu affairs commissioner because the government still sees black women as minors: and then they won't give us what rightly belongs to us. They want to keep it for us, tell us what to do, dictate terms to us. I refused to go to the bantu affairs commissioner, I flatly refused: and again asked my attorney to handle my affairs. They were really furious at the bantu affairs office – I had to go and tell the commissioner that the attorney would handle my affairs. I suppose I was insisting on modern civil law instead of tribal law. Finally they accepted it and I got my money from the bank.

'I've had no difficulty in my trade union work because I'm a woman; it has something to do with the fact that women have been active in all the trade unions except the old mineworkers' union from the very beginning – and we would have been there too, if we worked in the mines! The fact that we didn't carry passes before – not until the late fifties – had given us a freedom of movement which helped the organising work. The men were a bit afraid of getting into the trade union movement because of the pass laws; they thought they might lose their jobs and they were afraid their passes might be cancelled. Even today, in the distributive and clothing trades especially, there are more women organisers than men – we've kept the headstart!

'At home my in-laws are still very traditional: they think a woman's place is in the kitchen. But on several occasions I've demonstrated that I'm capable of doing what they can do. I shown them that I can maintain my house, that I can maintain my family without a man. Since my husband died I've taken no husband; I've been educating my children, staying with them in that house: and I've been doing better for them than other men are doing for their own wives in their houses! Now my in-laws don't try to tell me what to do any longer. . . .

'I can't compare myself with somebody from the Transkei, where they are still held down by tribal customs; yes, I can't compare myself with such a woman. She would have her in-laws coming in to the kraal and telling her what to do with her husband's cattle, you see. (And it would still be cattle, if there was any wealth at all, rather than money in the bank. Or perhaps a few goats or some sheep . . . cattle are becoming very rare. . . .)

'In my trade union work I feel very strongly that what we do is not only about improved pay and conditions of work for our members. . . . I can think of no country where the trade unions haven't taken a leading role in a liberation struggle. I also believe that when that day comes women must be full and equal – the struggle for one is a struggle for both. Discrimination because of sex must go as surely as discrimination because of colour. . . .

'We find when new members come in to the union from the rural areas they take a bit of time to get used to a woman trade union organiser – at first they won't listen to us! Until something happens to them, then they come running to the union and the woman will speak for them until they get what is rightly theirs . . . from there they'll start respecting a woman.

'In 1980 and 1981 we've had more strikes than usual and the mood of militancy seems to be growing. At one factory where they make petticoats, it was all women workers . . . that strike was successful. The women office-cleaners, who have to work at night and finish at two in the morning – they are members of our union. Some of them try to sleep at the station, others get on the early morning trains, but they have a dreadful time because they live so far from the city, and it's so dangerous at night.

'They're actually in danger of being murdered for the few rand they earn. We are working for an improvement in their wages and more reasonable hours; and – and this is crucial – we are asking the cleaning companies for a place where they can rest in safety when they knock off, and before the first trains run that will get them back to the townships. The wage determination that governs them is very low – they earn, mostly, about 100 rand a month.

'We aim to organise all the unorganised workers. We realise that women who are doing unskilled jobs are being exploited more than any other group. If you look at the office cleaners, they're a good example . . . and besides that, many of them are migrant workers, brought to Johannesburg and other towns on contract, which makes them even more vulnerable to company pressure.

'Employers today aren't keen to see our growth, but they're being forced by circumstances to accept it. When it comes to strikes, we're usually successful in linking up the workers and the employer. In the old days – they still try and do it on the mines – workers would just be dismissed or sent back to the tribal areas and new ones taken on: that doesn't work any longer, because of our existence.

'Black women workers have a major difficulty during confinement: they lose their length of service bonus, their seniority, and are expected to start all over again afterwards . . . even if they've only taken three months – unpaid – leave. Sometimes they even lose their jobs, until we get them reinstated.'

Emma Mashinini

Emma Mashinini is the general secretary of the Commercial,
Catering and Allied Workers' Union. It is an all-black union
which shares office space with its 'white' counterpart, the
National Union of Distributive Workers.

'I was a shop steward for about twenty years in the clothing
industry; and I served on the executive for twelve years . . .
that was in the Clothing Workers' Union, which was for the
black members of the garment industry – the whites and
coloureds were garment workers no. 1 branch and garment
workers no. 2. Even then we were divided into three tiers.

'It was partly as a result of the 1956 Industrial Conciliation
Act, which excluded black workers. Of course some white
unions accepted it in a different way – they took no interest in
organising the black workers: that wasn't the case at all with
the garment workers – we worked closely with them but were
legally divided to fit in with apartheid law.

'It's surprising, today, that there's such a big clamour for
organising black workers: those very same white unions who
had nothing to do with a black worker are today interfering
in the independent black trade union movement because
they're now extending their constitutions to include the
organising of black workers. Today it makes life easier for
them because they're more likely to get the firms recognising
their representativeness, so they register on this new basis.
Independent black trade unions don't have the same easy
access to management, or to the right to organise inside the
factory gate; but once a white union opens its doors to black
workers, they immediately have that access. They get pay
stop-order facilities – management is keen to see the
development of that kind of union; they much prefer them to
our independent black unions.

'Personally, I'm keen to see black workers in their own
trade unions because it's not honest – we are not being fair by
pretending that we want to be in the same one union. How
can we be in the same union, when there's no equality for us
before the law? A white union cannot cover the disabilities
that we suffer as blacks and as women, over and above being

workers. How can I sit in a meeting with white workers and discuss my pass – that I've been arrested for a pass offence on the way home from the shop or the factory?

'What we've done here in the distributive trade is to try and get the best of both worlds. We work closely with our white colleagues, although their union is separate. We even share an office and facilities. We share knowledge, we consult one another . . . but we just cannot be one union. They gain from us, we gain from them. . . .

'We also ask, who is the community, who is the worker? It's the same person, so we can't be interested in the worker only on the shop floor, and not follow, whenever they leave the workplace. If there's anything in housing, anything that affects them in transport, and anything that affects the community – it actually affects the worker.

'In those particular areas, wherever they are, our trade unionists have to speak both as workers and with the community.

'Speaking for myself – and I work centrally, not so much on local issues – I've never experienced any resentment from the men who are members of the union because I am a woman and I have a leading role. We have more men than women members – it's about 60:40 – so that's always pleased me. We also have an engineering union, which is mainly men, that's headed by a woman. Jane has been secretary of that union for many years, and the men have not rejected her. Most of our members work in shops . . . and we've met quite a lot of hostility from employers – it's taken many years for them to be prepared to sit down and talk. Now some of them are prepared to do that . . . we have been organising for years, but for a very long time neither they nor the government would recognise our work and our right to organise. People have been banned, removed, whatever, but the trade unions kept on mushrooming. . . .

'When it comes to my personal life as a woman I have tried to base it on mutual respect for the other sex. It's the same with race – we don't want domination of any one group by another; and it must be the same between the sexes.

'My daughters – they must never accept, or see themselves as inferior because they are women. It hasn't been a difficult thing to achieve at home. I live a full and active life. I'm active in my own community and in the trade union movement – if I don't go to something it's because I'm committed elsewhere, not because someone has said no. I don't know how the inner person is accepting it, but my husband – perhaps it's my approach. I never say, "Please may I?", but rather inform him of my plans. In fact we plan together; I think we always have. I really can't look back and remember anything different; perhaps it's because I've always been a working woman. It never mattered how little I earned – I always tried to come out on it.

'My mother didn't have an equal relationship with my father. But at the same time she wasn't the kind of person who would stoop low.

'We women are still minors in law, especially black women – but although others may see me like that, it's not the way I see it. I kick up enough row, like if I want to buy something on hire purchase, and when I'm told I can't purchase it because I am a woman – then I refuse to buy it. I even have a consultation with the woman's legal status group – then I tell the firm that I'm prepared to bring my husband along to sign as a witness, but that we have equal status. I'm not prepared that he should sign first and me after . . . it must be on *my* name if it is mine.'

Mary Ntseke

Mrs Ntseke, now an organiser for the General and Allied Workers' Union, talks of her life and her struggles:

'I'm born in the rural areas. I came to Johannesburg as far back as '48, started working in Sophiatown . . . but in 1953 I refused to go to school any longer, because the government began to instroduce bantu education. It's inferior to the universal education that we had before; I personally felt it was wrong for the children to be given a type of education that would draw their minds away from the standard that was equal and open, which we'd been teaching. I was 35 at the time. I was married, and I suppose what you might call politically aware. . . . I'd originally learnt about politics from Lilian Ngoyi, to join the African National Congress in the early fifties. In 1968 I was detained for forty-eight days. . . . I was left in the cell in ordinary gaol conditions: they would throw whoever they want to throw in there. The unfortunate thing was that you could not speak to anybody; there was nobody to talk to you, you were just isolated.

'Today I live in Soweto and do my trade union work. But in many ways things are made very difficult for me because we are mostly black members, and there's no freedom of speech. As a trade unionist, I don't have the right to walk in to a company and start organising the workers. I must wait outside until I get two or three coming out of the factory; then I can start telling them what a trade union movement is about. It takes a long time for me to get a few people in that particular firm. If I was a member of the white trade union council I'd have the right to walk into the factory, to make appointments with the employer or with the workers at any convenient time. As a black trade unionist I don't have that privilege. You also find, when you speak to an employer, that he'd be more satisfied if he were speaking to a man – that's the impression he gives.

'Within the trade union I have no difficulties because I'm a woman and an organiser. My colleagues treat me as an individual and as an equal – I think they respect me and there hasn't been any attempt, in our union at any rate, to keep women down because they are women. There are women who are supposed to be in the battlefields, as I am – you notice that these women's voices are not heard because, in some cases, they are not in a position to explain themselves, the way they should. And then the men don't listen. As an individual with so many years of experience in the trade union movement I don't have that problem.

'At home I must be a woman according to African custom. I must be under my husband's control all the time. He is the person to make suggestions . . . because I've grown up under that system I accept it; not that he really oppresses all the time. In some cases we sit down and discuss matters, and we settle them amicably. I do believe that there should be equality in personal relationships – but I also accept the more traditional way! I suppose it's easier for me because he's a reasonable man and doesn't try and take control of practically everything by giving instructions.

'I'm married in community of property. If my husband dies now, then I have control over everything that he has. It does give me, for example, the power to dispose of the goods if I want to.

'I could also take over our home in Soweto because it's in his name at the moment. The fact that I'm well aware of the bureaucratic tangles that the West Rand Administration Board makes at such a time – houses are so difficult to come by, and they might still try to throw me out – would also make it easier. It's just as important for a black woman to know how to fight as to have legal rights!

'In the past especially men have tried to overrule us, but in the city things have greatly changed. We are not against men. We work as equals – we are coming to a stage where generally things will be on a more equal basis.'

Liz Abrahams

Liz Abrahams was the general secretary of the Food and Canning Workers' Union in the Cape until she was banned from office by the government in 1963. Today she is secretary of her local branch in Paarl. The food and canning workers were organised on a racially integrated basis until 1947, when Department of Labour pressure forced them to form a separate African branch – and although this is still the situation today, the branches have always worked together on a close and equal basis. Mrs Abrahams gives examples of solidarity by black to coloured workers, and coloured to black, which helped each group improve their conditions of work. The Fattis and Monis strike she speaks of was accompanied by a popular, nationwide boycott of the firm's goods, and this was a further spur towards the reinstatement of the victimised workers.

'In the Western Cape the majority of our members are women . . . but if you go to Durban and Port Elizabeth then you get the majority is men again; mostly African men. We've always been a mixed union, both sexes, all races. And the men have always stood with the women, on any problem. The women too – they've shown the same solidarity to the men. From my time when I worked in the factory, you know, we would discuss together – there were committees of men and women together; there was never a problem. Whenever a deputation goes in to management, we are always mixed.

'I worked at Langeberg fourteen years . . . the employers did sometimes try to say, "This work is for women; this work is for men" – but we always ignore it. At the time, they were also not prepared to meet the Africans with the coloureds, whenever there's problems: this was in 1965 or '66 – at this stage they didn't want the African Food and Canning executive to come on the premises at Langeberg. So our executive discussed the problem and then they went in to the employers and they insist that the African executive should also come on the premises. Well, so we were successful.

'Now there's a lot of things that happen with men; and at first the employers are not prepared really to solve the problem but then they call in our officials, and most of the time we get the problem solved. I always say, "We just try"; we are taking a chance, OK, if you don't move further we have to leave it like that; but once you come to the officials then we go in there and most of the problems is solved.

'Our African members have far more problems – the employers apply to the black "homelands" whenever they need labour – thirty or forty from the Ciskei or the Transkei or wherever. They apply for immigrant labour and go down to the Transkei and bring them back on contract – it's men only, for six months or whatever they decided; when it expires they must go back and renew their contract.

'They gain strength from us, because we of couse are settled here and it's much easier for us to organise . . . now you see what happens: I'll give just one example of what happened at

Frappouw – there were immigrant labourers among the strikers at Fattis and Monis. We had really a hard fight to get them also to stay, while the strike is on. We went to the Native Settlement of Disputes offices; we had to go through a lot of things because they tried to send them back immediately.

'They had a court case, and the ruling in court was that they have to stay until the problem is solved.

'When it was all over the factory renewed their contract and they gave them a bus free to go to the Transkei and Ciskei to take their papers . . . and the employer let them all come up again. He employed everybody again . . . it was because of the unity of the workers, not because they had developed any particular skills in those six months before the strike.

'I call that an exciting strike. The workers were really determined, because five of the workers that were dismissed were coloured workers. The next morning all the African workers stood in the yard and they said, "We are not prepared to go to work unless we know what our coloured sisters did; and why they were paid off." This was in 1979 – the strike lasted seven months.

'We had to have meetings with the workers every day; and see that they get something to eat, and really, we did had a struggle to keep up with the workers' problems. More than a hundred were on strike – the majority were Africans. We had strike funds but they became exhausted – we had to appeal to other trade unions and the community . . . it was because of this financial support that we could keep the strike for seven months. When the agreement was made the workers were reinstated unconditionally. . . .

'I'm 54. . . . I must say I've never had any difficulty because I'm a woman and a trade union organiser . . . no resentment from the men . . . in fact there's a saying that women can explain things better to the workers than men!

'I grew up here in Paarl and we were eight children, four brothers and four sisters . . . my father was a sickly man; I had two brothers in the army . . . I was in the middle. I decided to leave school, so that I could help my mother; we just couldn't afford for me to go on. My mother worked in the factory when there was no union yet, and that's where I joined her. My younger sister stayed at home and looked after the younger children.

'I used to sit knitting outside when they were holding a union meeting; but soon I joined it! Later our president got banned – Fred Marquand; and then I got very worried – I couldn't figure it out by myself; why do they ban people? Then one day we had a management committee meeting and it was explained – and something grew up in me to say, "But why ban people? Why do nasty things like that with people? They're not criminals; they didn't kill anybody . . . why must they be so cruel to people?" And from then on I took a much deeper interest in the union . . . and later I was elected to a committee to take up complaints . . . we were struggling for better conditions and better wages. I wasn't married at that stage, so it was easier, perhaps – all those evening meetings. . . . Later, he was difficult about things when we got married . . . the union was growing quite fast; we spent quite a lot of time just fundraising. He became a heavy drinker; and I lost two babies with ectopic pregnancies – I can understand his problems; he was all the time alone; I was away Easter, Christmas – too much of the time. One day when I asked him, he said he couldn't bear the loneliness of it; he must sit at home with nobody while he saw other husbands and wives together.

'Later he got very difficult, in spite of me saying, "Come to the meeting; come and see why I come home so late." And then I made him join the Coloured People's Congress . . . you can see the reason why I always comes late. Then he joined, but after a few meetings he said, "That's not for me." Well, so I just left him but we still had a lot of arguments for a time . . . lately he decided not to interfere with me any more . . . he knew I'd never leave the union, and my busy-ness with it.

'In fact, his whole attitude has changed . . . he doesn't drink so much; and if I say I'll be coming late he even tries to come early himself so he can make a little supper for us. He grew to understand . . . usually, you find, men in such a situation turn to other women, but he never did; only the drinking when he got upset.

'I think decision-making should be something done

together in the family . . . and I really believe that when it comes to women in the struggle, then men should assist . . . he'll agree to see to the children if she's late from a meeting, put them to bed . . . and our political struggles are not the only reason. I think the children and the cooking are still the women's responsibility – the men should help, not share this.

'I want to see a free South Africa, where people can live where they want; they can work wherever they can get work – all discrimination would be gone. We shouldn't be represented by people who doesn't understand our struggles and our own hardships – we must elect our own people that can talk on behalf of us and that can represent us.

'There's no point having someone who hasn't struggled or known poverty, like these people on the President's Council who are supposed to speak in our name. These are people who have never eaten a bitter pill, who doesn't know about poverty . . . they cannot speak about it.

'And in terms of men and women – we do the same work but the wages are different – I think if the women got the same skill as men then they must be treated alike. We have been managing to get the gap reduced. Every time we meet the employers on wages we are trying to bring the gap together . . . in fact there are now a few women who are doing the same work as men who are getting the same money, but they're only the few. Say for instance you have a machine operator – he will get in the region of 70 rand a week; a woman, if she's a Grade 1 worker, she'll earn 60 rand. But that's because we've been demanding a closing of the gap. We want equal pay. Sometimes the husbands, too, don't want this equality . . . they won't let them come to meetings. . . . I had an argument with one of the workers' husband – "Look, why are we doing this: we're doing it for our children's future; we're getting old, leaving the industry, and new leaders must be built. And what your wife is struggling today is for your children's future, not for our own." I think it's also jealousness – they see their women mix with men. And one man said to me, "If she's going to be so active in the union then she's not going to listen to me any more."

'Even without a vote today, we can build the unity among workers: this is a power we can use, as we did in the Fattis and Monis strike. And there the unity was especially strong between the Africans and the coloured workers – they fought against our dismissal and we fought for their right to strike and stay; that success was a double success because we did not win only the right to reinstatement.'

Chapter 7

STUDENT REVOLT IN 1976

Education and its quality and content has proved to be as smoulderingly angry a part of the anti-apartheid fabric as the pass laws. In Lefurutse in 1956, and then in 1960, when police shot peaceful demonstrators at Sharpeville in the Transvaal and Langa in the Cape, hostility was overwhelmingly directed at the central aspect of the control mechanism – the pass itself. But in 1976 the immediate cause of anger, which again brought peaceful, disciplined and even hymn-singing demonstrators face to face with police who shot to kill, was an education of gross inferiority that was designed to reinforce the maintenance of a poor, ill-educated, pliant workforce, most of whom were expected to spend their lives waiting quietly in the rural wings for an opportunity to work in the more dynamic industrial economy.

Over many years, as with passes, there had been protests, boycotts, sit-ins and expulsions: schools and colleges were closed, students sent home, threats made and threats executed, so that an education was truncated here or aborted there. Young people were convinced then, as now, that their education was inferior. In 1979 71 rand was spent on every black pupil, 225 rand for a coloured child, 357 on an Indian, 724 on a white child. By 1982 the figure had not changed significantly – 1,000 rand for a white pupil and 113 rand for a black one; and pupil/teacher ratios continued to compare badly at 1:18 and 1:45. In late 1975 a young black, quoted in the *Natal Mercury*, said, 'The education given to Africans is so low that a Standard 8 pass with us is equivalent to Standard 6 for all the other ethnic groups.'

Perhaps even more telling is the fact that half of all black children actually leave school again within the first four years having barely started, and only one in a hundred get to the top form at high school. Teachers themselves have not usually been in the top form themselves. They teach in schools that may be icy shanties in winter, dark yet unendurably hot in summer. Books are a rarity paid for by parents and learning is based on the rote.

It was within this framework that a newly formed bantu education department began insisting, towards the end of 1975, that blacks at upper primary and lower secondary level should in future have some of their tuition in Afrikaans. The language is an even greater symbol of white oppression than English, used as it is by police, army and administrators. Its use in commerce and industry is confined to a minority – and it is not even a language with which most black teachers are familiar. The immediate response was one of outrage. Students, parents and teachers were unanimous in their hostility and in Soweto, by March of the following year, lessons were being replaced by debates on current affairs, discussions on black power or talks on the work of Martin Luther King. The debates were concerned with orderly change leading to eventual majority rule. By mid-May students had begun a stay-at-home; others stayed in school playgrounds as buildings were closed. The deep anger that had united everyone in the first place was to be expressed in a march and demonstration on June 16: by seven in the morning 15,000 young people were walking in orderly, good-humoured columns to the Orlando soccer ground. Then the leaders heard that the police were approaching the column.

Sophie Tema, one of the black reporters there, heard a youthful leader say, 'Please, brothers and sisters, I plead with you, remain cool and calm. We do not know what the police are after; after all we are not fighting. All we want is that the department must listen to the grievances of our brothers and sisters in the lower schools.' But in the mêlée that followed, four children were shot by the police and dozens injured.

Another reporter from the *Rand Daily Mail* said afterwards that he had not heard the police give any order to disperse, before they threw tear gas into the crowd of singing schoolchildren. . . . 'They scattered in all directions. Then they regrouped and the police charged, so they threw stones.

The police then fired a few shots, some into the air, others into the crowd. I saw four children fall.'

That was the start to heartbreaking weeks of violence and enormous tension between those who had begun by seeking a small, specific change in educational policy and those who, in their response to this modest demand, could only respond with brutal fury and fear. No matter that even an administration as rigid as this one eventually had to abandon the policy – in the meantime Soweto and eventually a great many educational institutions and black townships in other areas suffered the vicious martial law of bullet and gun. No one could say, after that first day, whether twenty-five or a hundred were dead, and as the weeks and months passed the toll rose and rose again. Strikes, demonstrations and stay-at-homes continued, sometimes the adults in a community joining the protest, sometimes not. Local issues were brought in – a strike for higher wages, at Mabopane near Pretoria, coincided with the students' refusal to leave the local high school. Buses, cinemas, administration buildings, beer halls and bottle stores were burnt to the ground, as well as the more immediate school premises. In Soweto, it was said that the bodies of young women and men were being thrown on piles outside the police station. Access to the local hospital, Baragwanath, was controlled by the police. Local doctors began treating the hundreds of wounded so that they would not be detained, questioned and gaoled.

The intention of this chapter is an elucidation of education for black pupils, but like urban life, or the special difficulties that confront women in South Africa, the topic is overwhelmed by apartheid, its weapons, its philosophy and its overweening control mechanisms in every sphere.

The events of Soweto during June and in the months that followed have not changed the educational system in spite of the fact that tuition through Afrikaans was abandoned. There are still four racially segregated departments of education. There remains the gross disparity of funding, the lack of sports facilities, libraries, outings – and the percentage of blacks who reach matriculation and can thus apply for skilled jobs remains at a third of that for all the other groups.

The government has said that all pupils now have the same

curicula. But a Unesco publication on South African history textbooks, *History in Black and White*, shows, in its painstakingly careful analysis, an overwhelming bias towards white cultural attitudes and white perceptions of the country's common history. It quotes textbooks where slaves 'became cheeky' and farmers showed 'intense indignation' about an ordinance at the Cape that introduced equality between white and black, textbooks that continually reinforce and legitimate values of racial superiority. The books are understandably suspect among black teachers. One young history teacher told me that she used them only as a guide, because it was essential to maintain the curriculum if anyone was ever to pass an exam.

'But really, they're totally unacceptable. I'd like to see one education system, a non-racial education. Just as a start, we must get rid of four sets that depend on the colour of one's skin. After that there'll have to be a sensitive recognition of different backgrounds, economic and cultural. It will be a huge and complex problem, but we must start from a non-racial standard. We'll get rid of these racist textbooks. . . .'

Apartheid may be at its worst in the rural areas, but it appears at its most grossly unjust in the schools: the children of Soweto understood that only too well.

Sibongile Mthembu

Sibongile Mthembu is 25 and has been frequently detained. She was a Soweto student in 1976 and was arrested in August and kept in gaol for three months. Since then she has spent four years in prison, and has now had a banning order placed on her that prohibits entry to 'social gatherings or institutions of learning'. She may not leave Johannesburg. Ms Mthembu has not seen her fiancé, who was also detained, for some time – he is no longer in South Africa. She is studying by correspondence to complete her schooling.

'I was born in Soweto. My mother worked here and there, sometimes doing domestic labour; at one time she was a nursing assistant. In fact, when she died she was a nurse assistant at Bara. . . . I remember my family as a Christian one – we had a Christian upbringing and my father is a lay preacher. Somehow or other we used to sit down and talk about things in general, as a family – we were six – we used to sit around and talk; we had this great interest in talking together. As a matter of fact, when you come to my place you won't know who belongs and who doesn't belong, normally there are a lot of people coming in and going out – it's an open house, which people like. So with so many people coming and going, you find your ideas broadening on many aspects of life. There were all sorts of discussions – religious, political. I was bothered, too, by a society that seemed more made for men than women – and in our society a man is traditionally higher than a woman. I used to query this as a child; I used to think, am I mentally retarded compared with him? Then as I grew up I realised it wasn't only a traditional thing – it was actually in law that we as women are discriminated against. My mother and father were resigned to this, much as they accepted all sorts of things, politically, that my brothers and I wouldn't stand for. They couldn't really dip down deeply into them, or encourage the discussions on a change in the system that we wanted.

'One thing though – I wasn't treated differently at home. My mother's attitude was the same to the boys and the girls: when it came to washing up, we all washed up. And when it came to education, we all had the same privileges – the four sisters with my two brothers.

'I was 20 and still at school in Soweto when the uprising took place in 1976. I was hostile to learning Afrikaans – not as a language but as a medium of instruction. I was arrested after the uprisings – I was arrested in August. There was a three-day stay-away being staged, and I was arrested on the second day at my sister's place. They didn't ask me any questions – when they came they were already hostile. They were armed as if they were going to capture a soldier, they had rifles. Then I was taken quite roughly, in my shortie pyjamas by the men – quite humiliating. I was taken to

Protea police station, where I was interrogated. They just kept me there and told me I was now being detained under Section 6 of the Terrorism Act. You don't have to be given the reasons why you're being detained.

'When the uprising came I thought it was something that had to come, because I had already believed for many years that I am entitled to the same rights as the people who are more privileged in this country . . . even as a child of 14 I had an attitude to the system, to the government, although it wasn't as strong at that stage because I was still a child.

'At the moment it's more important for me to fight for political rights as a black person . . . thereafter I might fight for my rights as a woman. But sometimes I think the two wars should go together . . . we have no option but to face the political struggle.

'I hope you realise that concentrated efforts on women's struggles and difficulties – say in the resettlement areas – also, in a way, is pushing up the struggle as a whole. When the woman suffers on the resettlement issue it doesn't only affect the woman, but the man himself. He doesn't like to see his wife suffering; he doesn't like to see women suffering; so even in him, he's got the spirit that he wants to fight for his women. The way I see it, at the present moment all blacks in South Africa, both men and women, have come together; and they want to fight this whole system as it is.

'The family is very important, too. To me the family can never be divided. The wife suffers – I take it the husband can feel the pains. And the children suffer – it is such a unit that it's not possible for one member to suffer alone, without the effects being taken over by the other members of the family. And that includes uncles, aunties, cousins – we have a feeling now for the whole nation, as one big family, and whether they're Zulu, Xhosa or what have you is quite irrelevant. It's irrespective of culture, custom – they're coming together now to form one big family.

'In marriage I think the best relationship is a democracy . . . we both have a say, we discuss everything and come to mutual understanding on things. I mean he shouldn't feel he's the head, that this is right just because *he* feels it. If I felt different from him he would always be open to criticism as much as I myself will always be open to criticism. As we are still minors in law, the only thing to do is to be wise enough to choose a man who doesn't differ from my ideas, otherwise I would be frustrated and it would be a disastrous marriage.'

Zuleika Mahommed

At the time of the students' revolt in Soweto there were solidarity strikes in many parts of the Transvaal, in Natal and the Cape province, mostly organised by black students. But in 1980 coloured high school students in the Cape, and also in Johannesburg, showed themselves to be in militant mood when the government organised celebrations based on the twentieth anniversary of Republic Day on May 31. Zuleika Mohammed was a pupil at the Chris. J. Botha Secondary School near Johannesburg then.

'There were thirty-eight of us – we'd locked ourselves into the science lab on the first floor because we wanted to show that not everyone was going to celebrate a Republic Day that was just another sign of our oppression. We went in on the Wednesday evening with sleeping bags, ready to stay for days, and with books so that we could study and fast. . . . Republic Day wasn't till the next Monday, but the government was in a panic about protests like ours, and they'd ordered all the schools shut and locked up, from Parliament.

'Before long the police arrived but we wouldn't let them in. They shouted at us but we ignored them – suddenly they broke a lot of windows and threw in tear gas . . . we were gasping for air, desperate to get out. I jumped out of one of the broken windows, but others opened the doors to run: there was an alleyway of policemen waiting for them, truncheons and sjamboks [rhinoceros hide whips] raised. Oh! we were cut and bruised from the glass and the fall, cut and bruised by the whips – we were all taken to the police station and charged.

'Eventually at one o'clock in the morning we each paid an

admission of guilt for trespass – except, that is, our head boy. Aziz was taken away by the security police and we didn't see him again for more than two months – they held him all that time.

'Everyone was very bitter – there was no question of anyone going back to school after Republic Day; for once teachers, pupils, parents – we were all united. We wouldn't go back – so then we organised a demonstration to protest about the detention of Aziz. Again the police attacked us, hitting, running, assaulting. There were at least 800 of us, but this was outdoors, near the Newclare swimming baths, and outdoor meetings are against the law – we were all charged and had to go to court. It was a terrible mess because they used tear gas again besides knocking the hell out of us; the smaller kids ended up in Coronation Hospital. Then we were all fined. . . .

'You can imagine what this does to school work. I was busy getting ready to write Matric, doing English, maths, biology, history, Afrikaans – but I'm working in a shop now, I just felt I couldn't take it any more. A lot of the others felt the same, what with the school being shut for weeks, a shortage of money at home. No point hanging about if the sick politics make the whole thing uncertain anyway.

'Before all this happened I'd decided I was going to train as a teacher. I mean – even under apartheid you can help kids find decent values; in fact it's a pretty essential job, isn't it, if this country is ever going to become a member of the human race? In 1976 we stood aside when things erupted in Soweto, only a few kilometres from here, but now coloured kids are becoming just as militant . . . in some ways, of course, we're better off – we can buy a bit of land right here so we can be more stable and secure. But most of us from Bosmont now feel we've got more in common with people in Soweto than with those whites with whom we share our language. . . .

'I'm sorry, now that I'm not at school any more, but I don't regret what we did. We were really united – Aziz is back at school, and he's chairman of the students' representative council. I don't think the police intimidation did anything except draw us all together in our anger. . . .'

Sheila Sisulu

Sheila Sisulu works for Sached – the South African Committee for Higher Education – which provides opportunities
for 1,200 black students to study for a degree through the
University of London.

'I grew up in Johannesburg – was born in Western Native
Township. I went to a mission school just at the time when the
government was starting the whole bantu education system,
where we were segregated from whites and others, as before,
but now had a new education that was considered
"appropriate" for blacks. There were immediate protests, and
in fact I remember being told by my brother not to go to school
because we were part of a boycott movement. I was only 6 or 7
at the time and I don't think I really understood what was
going on. There had already been demonstrations and
clashes . . . the day I stayed home was "D-Day" and all those
who didn't come were regarded as boycotting and
immediately thrown out. You could say I was expelled at the
tender age of 7! That was in the fifties. Congress set up
schools – makeshift schools in halls, and we had older pupils
trying to teach us. . . . I can't remember today whether it was
in English or Sotho! This went on for about about three
months, but then I was allowed back into my own school after
all; but of course the curriculum had changed . . . the
inspectors were coming around to make sure the teachers
taught in the children's mother tongue: we really started
getting the third-rate education that was supposed to turn us
into third-class citizens.

'Finally my parents decided they couldn't stand it any
longer. Slap bang in the middle of the school year they sent
me off to a mission school in Swaziland – they were fortunate,
because they could afford to do that.

'They really felt everything was collapsing around us – that
was true, certainly, for many of my friends. They never got
beyond a primary school education, and the little they had was
dreadfully poor. We had been seventy-five to a class before I
went to Swaziland – the teachers couldn't cope: they used to
try and force people to leave, to bring the numbers down.

'It's still happening now – when they talk about compulsory education these days for blacks, they don't prepare for it and at the beginning of each school year they have such an influx they're quite overwhelmed.

'School starts at 7 – you can't speak of compulsory eduction and then not provide the facilities. It links up with the peanuts that's being spent on black education generally; it may sound fine for the outside world, that phrase "compulsory education", but it doesn't mean very much when you see the desperately overcrowded reality.

'In Swaziland the classes were very much smaller and the teachers could really teach us something . . . after that I went to University in Lesotho to do a BA in English and philosophy, as well as an education certificate. When I came back to Soweto I began to teach in the high school – and found that numbers had grown to 150 pupils per class! Then the department decided I wasn't a fit person to teach anyhow because of course I'd learnt no Afrikaans in Swaziland or Lesotho. . . . That was in 1975, before the Soweto uprising; they said I could stay as an untrained teacher at a salary of 79 rand a month – I couldn't cope, so I looked for another job and left. But it was the numbers, not the money that decided me.

'The objection to bantu education is complex. Not on numbers, like me trying to teach 150 pupils the same thing, and not on money: it's very easy to see where the huge sums that go into white education are used. We only get a tenth of that, so parents have to pay for books as well as uniforms, when they can afford it. And of course when it comes to science courses it's quite impossible when you haven't got the equipment. All that is really straightforward – if the same amount was spent on schooling of every child in this country one of the objections to bantu education would go.

'In 1976 the language became such a big issue because it helped symbolise all the inferiorities. First the children start school learning in Sotho, or Zulu – then at high school they were told they had to learn through Afrikaans: it helps perpetuate the backwardness, the lack of education. . . .

'On paper the syllabus is the same for whites and blacks. But it has an enormous bias – the only thing that matters is what the whites have done. Black history either doesn't matter or else it's put across in such a biased way: blacks are cheeky, whites are good. When it comes to English you'd think there's nothing that can be changed; after all, if you're teaching a verb, what else can you do? But I had a comprehension passage in an English textbook that contained "Yes, master, berry quiet, berry careful." And that whole book was a translation from Afrikaans into English – it sounded really clumsy, not English at all.

'We're supposed to want mother-tongue education. Every sociologist and educationist says kids should first learn through the language they know . . . we believe that the only way to get an equal education today in South Africa is to see that it's in English from the word go. That's not only political. So many families see it as a tool to escape poverty . . . sons and daughters are sent to school for many years right into their twenties, in the hope that they'll reach Standard 5 or 6. Some of them have time off in the middle to look after younger ones – they go to school in rotation – but the belief that this can change lives is really powerful and many stick at it. They try and stay on at school in spite of huge difficulties – no money, nowhere at home to do homework in peace, not enough textbooks. And then, at school, undertrained teachers and hardly any equipment. In winter they work by candlelight in the evening.'

Chapter 8

A WRITER

The most incisive comment recently on apartheid and racism has been the play *Woza Albert* by Pecy Mtwa and Mbongeni Ngema. Racy and sharp in style, it is full of movement and vitality and uses the simplest of props (a ping-pong ball on the nose does for playing 'white') for the authors to enact their theme: when Morena, the good Lord, comes down to earth, what will the politicians make of him? When they have retired, covered in embarrassment, the play also provides an opportunity to celebrate the heroes and heroines of the democratic revolution they – like Nadine Gordimer, who is interviewed here – believe must come.

Watching the triumphant close at a performance in South Africa was to be enmeshed in noise; Luthuli – roar of applause; Lilian Ngoyi – a further roar; Bram Fischer – cheers. When the names of Biko and Mandela were added the sound cascaded from the theatre. This is immediate and readily accessible agit-prop, making sense of the apparently senseless and brutal present. At the moment it seems a form expecially well suited to the need for shaping relevant work, and its mélange of Zulu, Sotho, English and Afrikaans actually helps to bridge internal gaps and cultures: rooted in township life, it reaches out with a suggestion of common understanding, a common society. But there are many ways of inching forward within the persecuted arts, many writers who adopt very different ways of rediscovery about the present senseless realities of life.

Nadine Gordimer, who won the Booker prize in 1974 for her novel *The Conservationist*, and whose novel *Burger's Daughter* was at first banned, writes absorbingly about South Africa in a form well within the Western mainstream. Oswald Mtshali and Mongane Wally Serote use poetry, as did

Ingrid Jonker, and there are painters, sculptors and composers whose commitment takes many different paths.

Central to these artists is commitment. It is one that the world may recognise more quickly than the establishment powers of South Africa, whose bannings and censorship of the arts sometimes follows international acclaim; where it precedes it the censor, with a wriggle of embarrassment, has been known to undo again the knot that was so carefully tied. The novelist André Brink recently had the ban lifted on his first novel, *Looking on Darkness*, after some considerable time, just as his fifth was coming out. And then the unbanning was only partial, with the peculiar condition that only those who could read it in Afrikaans, and were over 18, were fit people to do so. ('The publishers', says Brink, 'will put a red band on it, saying, 'Only for those over 18'. Can you imagine anyone taking notice? But of course it might actually boost sales.')

Another playwright who has run the gauntlet of censorship, as well as having his freedom of movement impeded, is Athol Fugard. In a sense he has become the father of South African theatre much as Strindberg influenced the growth of drama in Europe earlier in this century; like the function Eugene O'Neill had in the United States: creating giant works while also having a seminal influence on those who were to follow like Tennessee Williams. When Fugard was finally allowed to bring his plays to Britain, Irving Wardle said, 'No playwright since Gorky has done more justice to the wretched of the earth ... of his plays that have reached Britain all carry the image of a rubbish heap peopled with characters who fear they may be rubbish themselves ... to audiences, at least, they are full members of the human race.' Fugard, who sees part of his job as 'bearing witness', has worked in close collaboration with two black actors, John Kani and Winston Ntshona, on many of his plays, but in essence they have remained his own construct.

Mtwa and Ngema broke that kind of mould by having the original creative drive themselves. In the shifting relationships between black and white artists, where people learn from each other by working together, by absorbing technique as well as substance, there has been a kind of turning of the tables here that seems a growth point: instead of Fugard supplying substance and Kani and Ntshona technique, Mtwa and Ngema have had both in abundance, but a white has been able to support by the polish of professional production techniques. It's difficult to speak of this kind of thing in South Africa because there is an understandably thin-skinned response to the notion that some skills, like certain cultural heritages, are still linked with ethnic background, but today's reality has become more like a mutual transfusion than a handing over of skills and material.

Nadine Gordimer, who draws absorbingly from very many different aspects of life in South Africa and beyond (I found one of her most gripping pieces of description in *Burger's Daughter* a passage based on the life of a small elderly community living on the Mediterranean), is deeply involved in a kind of continuing cultural exchange with young writers in South Africa, many of them black. She almost drowns in the amount of work she undertakes in this field, not considering it any the less important than her own writing and lecturing. Like Fugard, she is sometimes called 'just another white liberal' and – more recently – a white supporter of black consciousness. I don't believe the labels matter; and she illuminates, in this interview, the reality of how her consciousness grew.

Nadine Gordimer

'My parents were very different in their attitudes. My father was a Russian Jewish immigrant. I have to remind myself often of this when I'm judging him, as I did as I got older. He came to South Africa at the age of 13; he came to this country at the age of 13, poor, without knowing any English. He did have a relative with whom he could stay; but I think there are some people, when they have an experience like that when they're very young, it limits them. It also causes them to cling desperately to any security that they find. And, I suppose, to feel, "Oh well, nobody sympathised with me," and not to identify with other people having problems, oddly enough; he made a modest success.

'He became a small businessman in a mining town and my mother – she came from England at the age of 6 – joined him from a much more comfortable and secure background. There was no hardship at all for her: she went to school here and had no problem of acculturation. English was her tongue and there it was . . . and she was much more conscious of political problems. She was conscious of the fact that there was a great mass of people who were very – what she would have called – underprivileged. She worked all her life for the "charitable uplift" of blacks. She helped found a crèche for black children.

'I was influenced very much by my mother, and I saw it, as a child, from her point of view, but I didn't, as a child, carry it any further. There were poor children, who were happy to have my cast-off toys or clothes at the back door; perhaps they were the washerwoman's children . . . but it seemed to me that this was God ordained. . . .

'There were people who had toys and went to a school warmly dressed and then there were poor little children; but I didn't ask myself why: children don't, one accepts these things – you accept your parents' values. And the moral lesson was that you were kind and you gave things to people who had less than you had . . . but I don't think my mother ever carried it to its political conclusion; that it was really no good, in the end, handing out clothes or running crèches while the law remained the same. But she often talked quite strongly if anybody spoke to a black person in a nasty way; she would immediately get angry; and I remember her saying many times, – "They ought to remember that they are also human." But that was the key to her attitude – she did have the feeling that these were people like herself, but she accepted the law. On the other hand, she, and my parents generally, like so many other English-speaking South Africans, were very anti-Afrikaner, and kind of scornful.

'The business of relating the social conditions I saw about me to law or to any moral questions came to me from outside, from reading. When I was about 12 or 13 I had the run of rather a good library that belonged to a lawyer friend of my parents, and he had the sort of books I didn't come across in

the local library: he regarded himself as a socialist and I
started to read Upton Sinclair: I can still see that particular
edition on the shelf there. And I read *The Jungle*, and it had
quite an important effect on me, because for the first time I
thought about the conditions in the stockyards in Chicago,
and the way the people lived, and I began to think about the
men living in the compounds on the mines round about us,
and to ask myself questions; and to ask other people
questions. "Aren't they married, haven't they got any
children? Where are their homes? Why do they come so far?"
But that was only the beginning of it. . . . I should say that my
concern about the kind of society I was living in came from
outside, from reading, not from anything anyone told me or
that I observed at home.

'We had the classic Southern American or South African
situation . . . there was a woman called Lettie, her surname
was Mbelo: I realise it was unusual that we even knew her
surname, compared with others; but how couldn't we? She
worked for us for thirty-seven years. She was there as soon as
I became conscious of people at all outside my own family,
and she stayed with us all through our childhood. She was
allowed a lot of authority over the children: the idea that the
white child pushes around the black nanny certainly didn't
apply in our house because I would get a good smack from her.
When I was a child you often ran away from school, and I
remember being dragged to school by her, very strongly. She
was a very big woman. We were very fond of her . . . she lived
in appalling conditions: she didn't have a bathroom, and
there was no question of her using the bathroom in the house.
There was a strange mixture of intimacy, especially with my
mother – when my father died and the children left these two
really lived together; and indeed she died in my mother's flat
– my mother was holding her hand when she died: a very
close relationship indeed. But again there was this
extraordinary acceptance – I remember as a small child,
there were cups in the kitchen, and I remember being told,
"No, don't drink out of that", because those were the cups that
Lettie and her friends drank out of. And it didn't occur to me,
in my innocence you know – "What is she going to give me?
What was there on the rim of the cup that I didn't get when I

sat cuddled up to her on her lap?" This question of the cups remained with me very strongly . . . so there was this physical feeling.

'Of course it didn't go so far as to think, "Why didn't this woman have a bath?" You know, you'd be afraid of her because she's supposed not to be clean, but you don't provide the means of her keeping herself comfortably clean. Of course she *was* clean, but there it was – and this, I think, was a very average white South African upbringing . . . no direct unkindness, but this incredible contempt that was expressed in these small ways. Ninety per cent of whites have been used to that. . . .

'It's amazing how quickly you can change as an adult: I've often talked about it before as a second birth; I think that white South Africans – some never break out of this imprisoning shell but many do, and usually round about adolescence, I think. So that indeed, for my generation – the people who are middle-aged now – the generation gap had rather a different meaning: it was a revolt against parental attitudes as well as authority . . . social attitudes.

'I think that each individual writer writes from within himself . . . it's not to do with blackness or whiteness but with the differences between individuals; but there are areas of life which, because of the law, are closed to one or the other. There are certain experiences of white life that it's very unlikely that any black writer would know enough of to write convincingly and the same applies, only more so, to white writers. But that doesn't mean that I believe that white writers can't create black characters; and that black writers can't do the same with whites. It's like saying that men can't write about women; it's also quite contrary to the way writers get their material. It ignores the fact that although the law has kept us, in some ways very successfully, apart, there's an enormous area of life where, for 350 years, one way or another – on farms and in town, we have been rubbing up against each other in a vast area where our consciousness is intermingled.

'The way a writer is taken by a theme is the same; but obviously, if you live in a black township, and the orbit of your experience is mainly there – street corner sellers of

mealies; passing your working life jogging along on the back
of a coal cart with a sack over your head – if that is your
experience a theme from that way of living will take hold of
you. But the process is the same . . . whereas a young white
writer might have taken part in the flag-burning at Wits [the
University of Witwatersrand], so that that theme would take
hold of him: it's just a matter of what you take in, from the
material of the society around you. I don't think that a
particular attempt to get close to "the people" – you see this
with black writers – I think if it's a conscious attempt; if
you're looking to select things that will illustrate certain
points, then the writing is a failure; the plays are a failure. It
needs genuine inspiration: Goethe said, "You put your hand
deep into the life around you, and whatever comes up – that's
your material." If you go looking for a specific thing, you kill
it. You have to let it come to you, and then you have to find
ways to use it.

'I'd like to see one South Africa, a real democracy. I don't
think that any of the existing political dispensations fulfill
that. You can't have a democracy if you have guarantees for
minorities; I think if you're to have special rights guaranteed
for whites, you're singling them out for ever – quite apart
from the principle involved, I think it's a great mistake. You
can see it going to happen in Zimbabwe, that some whites
cling to the idea that they've got a guaranteed number of
parliamentarians representing them as a group. I think this
is perpetuating the old hurts and frustrations and hates of
the past. There has to be a tremendous element of trust when
great change comes about; and I think that's the hardest
thing for us whites to learn here. It's almost a kind of
Pascalian wager, you know – that you have to assume that
there's going to be a humane society here, because if you start
assuming that there won't be, and having these minority
guarantees, you're just perpetuating the problem.

'I think, as far as black women are concerned, that they'd
agree that at the moment they're in the struggle – there's no
time to think of the other struggle that's going to come
afterwards, within a black society – for women to come into
their own. I think that was one of the side effects of the
crushing of the mass movements, where the emancipation of

women from their doubly second-rate state – firstly as black
and secondly as women – was beginning to come about
naturally within the movements. Women were big and
important in the old ANC, a real force. People like Lilian
Ngoyi were really very special; but when the movements
were crushed and when they emerged underground in a
different form somehow there was less place for women; they
became supportive again. One's seen it again in the rise of the
black consciousness movement and the children's revolt of
'76 – the mothers were tremendously supportive, and
somehow very quickly politicised by their children, but if you
look back twelve or fifteen years you realise how much
ground black women have lost in South Africa since the mass
movements were banned.

   'But I think black women are not only terribly important
on the political side – but also in the cultural role. Mitterand
has said recently that he sees socialism as a cultural problem.
I think black women are close to the young in the black
consciousness movement in that they see the emancipation of
blacks, black freedom, not only as a political and one might
almost say military problem, but also as a cultural one. In
their homes, in their . . . in values, that's what I mean, in
human values . . . they are extraordinarily strong – I often
feel myself in awe of this tremendous spirit of black women. I
remember – oh, long ago, it must have been fifteen years ago
– I was at a political trial. A black man got twelve years, and
his wife jumped up in the gallery and she shouted, "Twelve
years! It's nothing, my husband!" It was incredible – and she
meant it. The way they manage to carry on – even in highly
politicised families. The husband's in exile; a child
disappeared in '76, has gone, is perhaps in Swaziland and
then goes off still further; perhaps hasn't been heard of for
some time – it's incredible, the courage with which they carry
on.'

Chapter 9

WOMEN IN POLITICS

All those who have spoken in the preceding pages have found their lives enmeshed in the rituals and realities of apartheid: without exception, they cannot work or buy a loaf of bread, get on a bus, get married or go to school without coming up against the barbed wires separating black from white, injustice from democracy and opportunity, hunger from plenitude. There are those, like trade unionists Emma Mashinini and Rita Ndzanga, who have endured torture, detention without trial, lengthy periods in gaol that stretch from weeks into months and years. Others, neither political nor trade unionist, have stumbled into the same net. But those who talk of their lives in this section have chosen, consciously and carefully, to take a stand. Sheena Duncan is a pacifist with a commitment based on her profound Christian belief; Winnie Mandela has felt, since her imprisonment in 1969, that she would now carry a gun if it were necessary. They spend their lives in struggle, like their trade union colleagues – a struggle that does not cease when they are banned, banished, gaoled. It is a commitment based on belief and political philosophy rather than skin colour or background.

When I went to see Mrs Sisulu she had been released from a banning order only two days earlier – an order that had prevented her from speaking publicly ever since her husband, Walter Sisulu, was first sent to Robben Island penal colony in 1964. Since then, she has been banned yet again, and also charged with furthering the aims of the banned African National Congress. I found her indomitable, warm, cheerful and caring; there was no trace of bitterness. She had been detained in gaol in 1963, as was her eldest son Max. Her daughter Lindiwe left South Africa in 1977 after a year in prison; her son Zwelakhe was detained under Section 6 of the Terrorism Act, a section notorious for its use in every and any situation.

Mrs Sisulu has lost none of her hope that there will be change, nor her aspirations for a better life, but still she says, 'All we're used to here at home is gaol.' There were 152 people in detention without trial when she said that, and a further 161 had had banning orders placed on them so that they were isolated from working and campaigning: both those numbers continue to grow inordinately.

Those who have been actively involved in the work of the now-banned African National Congress have taken their place within a tradition that began to crystallise as the present Nationalist government came to power in 1948. Then young men like Sisulu, Oliver Tambo and Nelson Mandela began calling for a new programme, and for the attainment of freedom and self-determination through a struggle that was no longer to be polite, moderate and restrained. Boycott, strike and civil disobedience were demanded in place of the pointless parleying of the old Native Representative Council on which the ANC had served. In 1952 the largest campaign of civil disobedience yet to be organised, the Defiance Campaign against unjust laws, took place amid mounting arrests, raids and bans on individuals. More than 8,000 people of all colours went to gaol that year for defying unjust laws, with Mandela as volunteer in chief.

In December of that year Albert Lutuli became president of the African National Congress: 'Who will deny that thirty years of my life have been spent knocking in vain, patiently, moderately and modestly at a closed and barred door?' he said. He was to win the Nobel prize for his work in the cause of world peace later on, but the new Nationalist government, spurred on by dreams of a final solution that resolved everything according to pigmentation and the curliness or otherwise of one's hair, arrogantly, brutally, did not listen. At the same time, the ANC was done forever with plaintive knocking at the door, and in a year its membership rose from 10,000 to 100,000.

Many of the new members were women. Annie Silinga, who joined then, was one of those arrested in the abortive treason trial of the mid-1950s. Lilian Ngoyi joined the ANC Women's League and by 1956 had become president of the new multi-racial Federation of South African Women that had a similar cause. (Ms Ngoyi, a woman of sparkling personality, a dedicated organiser and stirring speaker, endured years of privation, banning and 'house arrest' – confined at home for twenty-four hours a day, unable to see even relatives and friends – yet before her death in 1979 she said she was still 'looking forward to the day when my children will share in the wealth of our lovely South Africa.') In 1956, as the police and army began their horrendous campaign to force black women to take passes, she – with others like Helen Joseph and Amina Cachalia – helped organise the huge protest demonstration at the Union Buildings in Pretoria.

By 1960, when more peaceful protest against the pass had led to the shooting of hundreds, and the death of sixty-nine men and women at Sharpeville and more at Langa in the Cape, the number of women involved in direct political action had become a considerable part of those working – as the Lutuli-era slogan had it – for One Man One Vote. Not all came from the cities and certainly many thousands were members of other organisations, like the Pan African Congress (which had its expression later in the black consciousness movement that began with Steve Biko), but the congress movement expressed most clearly the aspiration for a free society that would share the golden toll that sunshine, gold and plenty could bring.

In 1960 too, hard on the heels of the largest demonstration by blacks that had ever been seen in the country, when 30,000 men and women marched into Cape Town in protest both against passes and the killing at Sharpeville and Langa, South Africa became a republic.

In that republic the African National Congress and the Pan African Congress were banned organisations, but until his arrest in August 1962 Mandela continued, underground now, to organise – this time for a national conference of those concerned with freedom. Later, at his first trial in 1962 and then the subsequent one in 1964 where he and his colleagues were sentenced to life imprisonment (at the Rivonia trial), it became clear that the ANC had advanced beyond Lutuli's fresh firmness of intent. Mandela told the court that the government itself, in anticipation of peaceful African protest and demands for change, continually 'set the scene for violence by relying exclusively on violence with which to answer our people and their demands.' In such conditions one could only submit or fight – and a branch of the ANC had been formed that would, from now on, fight.

In the years that followed, repressing of all those who worked for votes and rights was draconian. Even where organisations were not banned, so many of their leading participants were prevented from working that the groups became ineffectual. Others, like the Liberal Party, decided to go out of existence rather than conform to new discriminatory, divisive legislation. It was a time for endurance and courage during which – as George Bizos says earlier – the burden of possible action fell heavily on women. It was not until the cloudburst of passion and fury that was Soweto in 1976 that the lull came to an end, although, during the whole period, the black trade union movement had continued to grow.

Since 1976 the growth of women's action, like that of the trade union movement, has been powerful – at the grass roots, as in Crossroads, in support of trade union action like the Fattis and Monis strike, and in the development of fresh activity by the Federation of South African Women and the United Women's Organisation. The government, alternating between wariness and its more typical viciousness, does not always respond consistently.

During this period, and until quite recently, the economy has continued to grow. At the slightest sign of difficulty – like a fall in the price of the gold that has always been the backbone of that growth – the International Monetary Fund stepped in, backing the government with millions of rands. Since 1984 the economy has gone into a severe recession. The growing demand for full equality, coupled with violent police and army repression, has led to major disinvestments by international companies and a growing inflation. In the past eighteen months international bankers, as well as the governments of the West, have become openly critical of apartheid: they now demand political change before they will go on lending money. And while white household incomes average twelve times that of black, a tiny percentage of the population live inordinately well, and the rest struggle to eat and survive. The link between money, power and rights and the government's interpretation of them has been shown most recently in the restructuring of the republic's constitution: three assemblies – white, coloured and Indian – with a diminishing say in the executive depending on skin colour. Blacks may continue to pound on the door, but have no chance of entering.

The women who speak here, however they see the way forward, are clear that it is to the question of power, and power-sharing, that the people of South Africa will finally have to address themselves. They are on freedom's side, they have the support of the world outside, but at home the gains remain small, the pain great and at times overwhelming. Yet I believe that those who speak here, like those who have gone before, have a degree of courage, and of resolution, that will ensure their strength be enough to win the day.

Albertina Sisulu

Albertina Sisulu is a former president of the Federation of South African Women. Her husband Walter is serving a life sentence on Robben Island and in Pollsmoor gaol as a leading member of the African National Congress, and her son Zwelakhe was detained as a result of his work with the Media Workers' Association. Mrs Sisulu was banned for seventeen years from joining in any public or political work; from social gatherings – even from going out in the evening – and more recently, she has been in gaol on a charge of furthering Congress aims.

'We went to Pretoria in 1956 to protest about passes for women in a group of women of all races – there were 20,000 of us, and in spite of losing that battle we gained in solidarity and strength. Of course we were forced into taking passes finally: the government said, "If you don't take the dompas, you can't stay in the town and work, you can't get your pension"; you couldn't live . . . so we had to, eventually.

'I was born in the Transkei, in the Tsomo district, so I'm a Xhosa originally. But I've been in Johannesburg since 1939. . . . I was just a girl from the rural areas when I met Walter, training at the hospital: he helped me to an understanding of the poltical situation – he used to relate what had gone on at meetings to me.

'I'd like to see a multi-racial South Africa where everybody's going to be free; free to speak, free to move and free in every respect. And that includes women in everything – there's no difference. Here in Soweto women are reaching an equal basis with men, and the men understand that – so when we struggle for rights we are automatically including rights for us women in that struggle. Some of the men – a few here but of course more in the countryside – don't understand this yet; most are no more the bosses.

'On the whole, women cope better than men when they become single parents. They work for their children; we have men who are "impossible", if you like, who will not work, who depend entirely on their wives – even that burden many women have to handle with a smile!

'Women are taking far more responsibility for the upbringing of their children and for their education, than the men . . . indeed, the struggle for the daily survival of their families, during the dreadful resettlements, when the men are away or when they won't help, falls on us women.

'Walter was sentenced in 1964, and just a few months after that, I was banned. I've seen him often – he looks very well, younger than me. But I've one thing I can boast about – my hair! His is just as white as a white beret whereas I've still got lots of black! I've been fortunate because all the time that he was on Robben Island and I've been banned, I've never been without work. I've been with the City Health Department for thirty-six years as a nursing sister – a midwife and a general trained nurse. I work in Soweto – when I was banned they took me off delivering babies because that involved night work that I was no longer able to do, because I had to be home by a certain hour.

'When I was first put under house arrest, the City Health said, "Oh, that would be fighting against the government, we cannot keep you as matron of that area." But when they

heard of my conditions, they realised that meant I would
have no job at all, so then they said, "No, you have served us
all these years, we can't just throw you away like that; we'll
create a job for you." And they gave me a job. So I was put into
the Child Health department in town . . . and I'm still there.
And I'll get a pension at 65.

'The government is incredibly stiff about pensions – you
must have a pass; you must be a person who has been here for
more than ten years; you must qualify to be here, in
Johannesburg; and you have to go into many offices – to start
with you go to the social workers, from the social workers to
the native commissioners – and they determine your pension.
You get it once every two months. The process takes a long
time; some haven't got people to take them there; they're old
and they have no transport; it's difficult for them to board a
train – oh, they're having it hard . . . in the country it's even
worse, especially in those areas where the government has
handed over pensions to Matanzima, Tsebe, Mongope and the
other stooges: often as not, *they* just say the homeland's run
out of money, and even a pension once every two months
disappears. Then people really starve, because in the country
whole families depend on that miserable 66 rand every other
month. And just imagine – women of 65 and over desperately
going out to look for any work that's going, in order to get a
few pennies or even just some crops and payment in kind.
There is starvation in the rural areas. . . .

'There's a great deal that we as women could do together.
At the moment we're thinking of more crèches – we don't
have enough for all the children; and their conditions do not
suit every parent. We have crèches that take our children at
2, whereas a parent will go back to work when the baby is
about two months, because there's no income. So we're
thinking of such crèches, where the babies will start much
younger, to help the mothers. When I retire that will be just
the work for me . . . and we have friends who will help us get
the money: white, black – mostly women. There are already
quite a lot of self-help nurseries in the townships around
here.

'There's an even greater difficulty than the lack of
nurseries – it's housing. Women have no place to stay. Even if

they are working for their children, it's difficult – sometimes you hire a room, and the next thing, when you come back from work, the children are in the street: the owner of the house has given the room to somebody else, just because of a minor quarrel perhaps. You might have been late in paying your rent, so you're chucked out of that room. The pressure to find a place to live – any place – is just enormous in town.

'In the countryside you can at least build something with corrugated iron, here we're stopped by the police and the shacks torn down. But there's no work to be had out there, and very little chance left to grow anything . . . here there's the chance of some work, and terrible pressure on housing; there it's real starvation. . . .'

Helen Joseph

Helen Joseph sits in her small house in Norwood, Johannesburg, surrounded by the mementoes of thirty years of hard work and struggle for human rights in South Africa – those mementoes, it needs to be said, that have not somehow found their way into the back of a police van during a raid or a search for banned or incriminatory material. She has been gaoled, banned, confined to her home for years on end, arrested, charged with treason . . . it has never stopped her from organising, boycotting, demonstrating, speaking and writing in support of her beliefs. Today at 79, she is a bit more frail than she was in the past but as buoyantly full of her passionate belief in freedom and justice for all, in the country of her adoption, as she was during the march to Pretoria in 1956 to protest against the imposition of passes for black women; and as she was in 1960 as one of the thousands detained for months after the shooting down of peaceful demonstrators in another anti-pass campaign at Sharpeville.

Her work as a national organiser of the Federation of South African Women, as well as that in the trade union movement – among garment workers – has brought her in contact with thousands who have never forgotten her warmth and vitality, as well as the egalitarianism that has informed it. Over the years her refusal to budge, to leave her chosen cause and go into exile, has brought her support, and love, and help from men and women in every group in a diverse South African society. Her long and close friendship with Winnie Mandela (whom she calls her adopted daughter) is a good indication that Ms Mandela's conviction that she could shoot whites, if necessary, has more to do with oppression and exploitation than skin colour. Helen Joseph has spent time in gaol for refusing to answer questions about a supposed visit to her banished friend. She was born in Sussex and has lived in South Africa since 1931.

'I'm not as concerned with people's political labels as with the struggle, and with people. . . . I came back to the church in 1966, and shortly after I'd been unbanned the Dean of Johannesburg came to my Christmas party. He sat on the ledge of the wall over there, and he looked at the thirty or forty people who were here, and he said, "Hmmph – Christians, Communists, Hindus, Muslims, Jews" – he summed it all up. . . .

'I came here from India in 1931. . . . I'd lived there three years . . . and the shock of apartheid nearly destroyed me initially, because I'd been in Indian India, not British India, and I couldn't bear it. But let me tell the truth, it wore off; I got used to it, and I enjoyed my social life; I married a dentist here. I always wanted to be friends with Indians, but Africans I saw as a strange sort of people. Then the war came, and I joined the Information Service . . . that's where I learnt, because we had to lecture on current affairs and on politics; and in order to be able to lecture I had to learn first. Then I began to see the facts – you know, the facts about bantu education; the facts of the discrimination; the facts of housing – and that began to worry me. I always had a bit of a social worker's conscience . . . that's where I started, but then, when the war was over I went to work in the Fordsburg Community Centre, among whites, and I began to think a bit more.

'Then I went to Cape Town, and went to work among coloureds, also in community centre work, and that was when I really began to get the message. I worked hand in glove with them, building from the grass roots, creating a centre; and it dawned on me that all I was doing was giving an aspirin for a toothache – and that lots of people could do that: that's what social workers are for, to give aspirins for toothache.

'I came back to Johannesburg and worked in the Garment Workers' Union – I learnt an enormous amount from Solly Sachs. . . . I kept feeling, "I must get into the political field; but what was there?" There was nothing. . . . Solly used to talk to me about the Labour Party, and I used to shout at him and say, "Well, the Labour Party's only concerned with white workers." Then one day he said to me, "Stop moaning about it – get into it and do something about it." I did, but only slid through – I really couldn't find a political home in the Labour Party. And then came the Congress of Democrats . . . the Liberal Association, at the time, wouldn't accept the universal franchise, and here was a body that would. I was invited to be on the provisional committee; by that time my convictions were there – that the only thing to do was to change the system.

'So it was a process; not one dramatic event but a ten-year process. But the attempt to recruit whites into the Congress of Democrats wasn't all that successful: we were faced with a bloody impossible task. We were the only ones who could do it: it wasn't for us to take the easy path and go recruiting blacks . . . so it was very small, but very real – a potent ginger group. I firmly believe that the Liberal Party would never have got as far as it did, if it hadn't been for us. We were always one step ahead of the Liberal Party. When it came to the Congress of the People they didn't want to come in because they hadn't been consulted at the beginning; we were in – we pushed them into adopting the universal franchise: they couldn't rule it out, because we were there. I think as a ginger group we were very effective . . . and we did have a symbolic value too. Here was one group of whites standing foursquare with the African National Congress, the Indian Congress and the coloureds. The congress alliance itself was tremendously important; and weren't we privileged to be a part of it? I think so.

'I've had nine years of total house arrest since the early 1950s – twelve-hour house arrest; then I've had nine years of freedom, but I'm still listed, so it's only partial freedom. But even so, I've addressed sixty meetings in nine years, and that's not bad . . . what meetings! I've had the most wonderful reception . . . it seems to be something that's appealed to everyone – the sight of an old woman saying, "Bugger the government!" And then they slapped this last ban on me. . . . I admit I earned it . . . treat it as an accolade anyway, an award of merit. I haven't been wasting these nine years. I think they were scared to do it before because they always hoped I wouldn't live that long. And I'm sure that's why it's only two years . . . we needn't put a five-year ban on her; she won't last that long! And it'll look better if she's not actually under a ban. [In 1971 Helen Joseph had treatment for cancer.]

'But I know what brought that ban on – they had a meeting in Durban; the Natal Indian Congress called a protest meeting to protest against the detention of their leaders. They were all scooped up and detained in June last year; they called me down to Durban to address the meeting: and there were 5,000 people there! Mostly young, and I was the last speaker . . . by the time I got to them they were already in a highly excitable mood; I could have said anything. . . . I did, I said all the things I wanted to say. And I ended up by saying my message to the detained is, "We shall overcome – will you sing it with me? I can't sing"; and they did – 5,000 voices sang "We shall overcome". I think they sang 5,000 verses, as far as I can remember . . . and that nine years of freedom was full of this: the young are such a wonderful audience, they really are. They give you their hearts. I was never much of a public speaker before. . . . I think it was the four years on the treason trial, the months in detention in the sixties, then the nine years under house arrest. I suppose all this is deep in my own experience, and it has given me, in some unexplainable way, the power to hand it on to others from the platform.

'My speeches are not ideological at all; rather highly emotional . . . real rabble-rousing! I've got my own ideas, but I've never been an ideologue.'

Then she spoke of the work undertaken over many years to try and keep a record and help the hundreds sent into exile –

banished – by the government. Banishment is an especially fiendish form of punishment for those unpopular with the apartheid regime because, like imprisonment, it can – and does – go on 'for ever'. But – and in this it is like a banning order – decisions on banishment are not made in a court of law according to known and established criteria; they are made administratively: decisions made in secret against which the recipient has no legal or any other weapon. With a banning order normal life is disrupted by restrictions on work, on where a person is allowed to go, whom they may see, when they can be away from home and how often they have to report to a police station. With banishment the system of control is compounded by sending people – and they have usually been black – as far as possible from their home, their piece of land and their family.

'Banishment under the old Native Administration Act of 1927 . . . there was an uncle and his nephew living up in Bushbuckridge, Acornhoek, way up in the Northern Transvaal – and they were both banished, because they were involved in disputes with the government about the Shangaans. These are Southern Sotho people, and the Shangaans have come in from the east, and there are tremendous disputes about the land that was given to them. These two men were leaders of their community, and they were saying the Shangaans had taken their land: it was a tribal thing. So these two men were banished; the uncle was Laynas Mqshile – they were taken to the Transkei, 1000 miles away, where the language was strange. One was taken to one Trust farm, one was taken to another. All right, after about ten years Wineas was allowed to go home; he was the less rebellious of the two; but Laynas wasn't – he remained seventeen years in the Transkei. Laynas was at Lady Frere. Now when the Transkei got "independence" you got the most ridiculous, absurd comic opera situation. Here is a man, who is not legally allowed to put his foot anywhere in South Africa, who has been banished to Lady Frere, but Lady Frere is now part of an independent state. It was the most absurd situation: he tried to get it clarified; he wrote letters and letters but never got any satisfactory answers. Finally he

said, "I'm going home." So he went home at the end of
seventeen years; the Transkei people said, "You can stay
here if you want to," but he went home. In the meantime his
people at Acornhoek had built him a beautiful new house,
against the time they believed he would come home. It was a
big house, and he had sent them all sorts of timber from the
Transkei, and they'd built the house and his wife and his
children had moved into it. They had never moved to the
Transkei, but had visited him occasionally. They *had* to stay
behind. . . . I interviewed his wife; she had to remain to look
after the lands, otherwise they would have lost their lands.
All the wives of the banished men stayed behind – people
don't seem to understand this.

  'Then, about two years ago, when he got back to
Acornhoek, by that time there had been a dispute about the
house that had been built for him, and his wife – she's a tiny
little woman – had been ordered to demolish the house. She
refused, and at the end of a month the officials came and
demolished it for her. . . . I've got a picture, just bits of wood
left of the beautiful house that had been built for his return
. . . that's what he went back to.

  'And when he got back he went straight to the
Commissioner and said, "Look, I'm here, I want my position
sorted out; my banishment order says I may not be here, I
may only be in Lady Frere – but Lady Frere does not belong to
South Africa. So where can I set my foot in South Africa?" He
was allowed to stay there for a year, and then he was
rebanished to somewhere in the Pietersburg area . . . can you
believe it? After seventeen years away, his home demolished,
he gets back for a year, has another child – the letter he wrote
to me, "We've got such joy, we've got a little daughter" – and
then he's banished again.

  'I must pay tribute to Helen Suzman – she took up the case
in Parliament, and finally got them to agree that he could go
home and not be harassed any longer . . . but it's a dreadful
story. A dreadful story . . . but what a man; what dignity. He
was an ANC man, he served a turn on Robben Island in the
very early sixties for his support of the ANC, and his courage
has never left him. His wife, a gentle, sweet person – she
doesn't speak English; I had to do all this with an interpreter.

But he's still on probation, a year at a time: his banishment order has not been rescinded – it still exists on paper.

'I think Chief Mopedi had the longest banishment order: he was one of the very early ones – in 1952 he was banished; he died eventually in about 1973.

'I suppose we've managed to help about seventy to eighty banished people . . . they showed such courage. Only a couple of women were banished. Rita Mopedi, the wife of the chief; they were from Witzieshoek. The other one was Mokwena Matlala, who was banished to Kingwilliamstown: she was the chieftainess of the Matlalas. There was a third woman . . . Seopa . . . I can't remember her first name . . . we tried to visit them all and maintained a massive correspondence. The sad story of the Matlala chieftainess was that she eventually went back to the Matlala reserve in the Northern Transvaal, and succumbed to government pressure. Mrs Seopa wasn't so politically minded herself, but oh! how she suffered. . . . I don't know if I'd be able to hold out against all those years of loneliness, waiting, waiting, waiting. Because there is no end to it; it's totally at the state president's discretion – the minister claims that all these cases are reviewed every year. And certainly, when Helen Suzman was trying to get some satisfaction on Laynas Mashile, certainly she did get his case reviewed every year; and every time it comes back with the same answer: "Seeing that the circumstances that led to his removal still prevail, it is not possible to consider his being allowed to go home again." Isn't it incredible? This is part of South Africa's unkown history.'

Amina Cachalia

'I was banned for fifteen years – it started in 1963 . . . November, and it went on till 1978. The first five years were absolute hell because the kids were small; they were at primary school and they needed me to go to school with them, to go and see their teachers, to have little birthday parties at home . . . that part really worried me the most. I could manage with not being able to see anyone because of my banning order; even with not going out – but I was very upset with the way it affected *their* lives. I was cut off completely from all other friends, relations, my sister and brother-in-law were banned as well. . . .

'I was only allowed to see three people while the banning order lasted – one at a time. If there were more than two people it was a gathering and against the law; and of course Yusuf was under house arrest, which meant no visitors at all except a doctor when he was ill. It meant that I was virtually under house arrest, because if I did have a visitor the police could easily have said it was someone who'd actually come to see him – it would have placed him in great jeopardy.

'To begin with I did all sorts of things: I cooked madly for a while – for two or three weeks I just went crazy and got myself busy in the kitchen. Yusuf just read and read and read . . . suddenly I couldn't cook any more; he couldn't read any more and we stopped . . . at least our livelihood was not affected because we were allowed to work in the shop: it was a relief to be able to talk to people about anything at all! So we saw each other every minute of the day – we were the most drawn together husband and wife team for that period. I saw him day and night, every day. I thought it might create tensions, I was very worried about that – I really thought that might be it, being with him night and day, not having any other people to be friendly with: gee, there goes my marriage one of these days, I thought . . . it didn't. Touch wood, it just didn't. It threw us together and we did a lot of things together – scrabble, patience. He couldn't go out at all, and I could only go alone, not with friends, so we stayed home together.

'If I did go to a movie or a theatre occasionally, my friends would sit in the rows behind, so that I didn't feel too completely alone. . . . I must have been 17 or 18 when I was first drawn into political activity; my family had always been involved. My dad was the chairman of the Indian Congress during the Ghandi period – he'd taken it over when Yusuf's dad died: you could say it was in the family. Really, politics was our whole life . . . as a kid I tagged along to meetings with my cousins and brothers and sisters. I was certainly very clear about our stand for equal rights and opportunities.

'In 1946 the Indian Congress began the passive resistance campaign: we were very much in the tradition that Ghandi had helped forge when he worked in South Africa. I was too young to be allowed to go to gaol, but I canvassed and did what I could. The struggle was meant for Indians, and appealed to them as a group, but at the time our unity with the African National Cngress was already quite strongly established, and a few Africans did join in. Our co-operation grew from then, until by the time of the Defiance Campaign in 1952 we were really altogether. Indian women were involved in these struggles from very early on. Even in the very first passive resistance campaign – the one organised by Mahatma Ghandi – an Indian girl died just after she came out of gaol . . . a girl called Vallia Mamoodlia. She was only 16. There were lots of others that went to gaol during that time. . . . Indian women have always played a role in the political struggles. They were as active as the men, but the men remained the leaders. So they were still suppressed . . . it's only recently that Indian women have gone out to work; they were always economically dependent on their husbands. Now they are becoming much more free, feel they can be their own boss, earn their own living. Like the men, we are hindered by all the discriminatory laws of the country, and especially by the Group Areas Act that means we can't live and work where we please. But otherwise, as women, there is no legal discrimination against us that doesn't also affect the men.

'There's a hierarchy of discrimination in this country . . . if you look at education you mustn't just compare what is spent on white children and black children: we fall somewhere in between, getting considerably less than the whites and a bit more than the coloureds and Africans. It's just a duplicate of the way the whole system works . . . everything based on degrees of discrimination.

'Even in the small things, where the government says that discrimination has now gone, it's not true. I can't play tennis today wherever I want to on municipal fields, I can't swim where I like – while they tell the world that apartheid no longer exists in sport!

'Young women growing up today don't accept the really

close family structures of the past . . . some families still carry on with the old traditions, but many of the young women have become really independent. They either work or study . . . even if they're married, they still go out to work today because the economic set-up has become so tight, the cost of living rising by the day . . . living out in a group area like Lenasia is twice more expensive than living in town where you're nearer everything else, where your transport facilities are easier . . . discrimination makes life more expensive for Africans as well – food costs more in the townships than in town.

'Although Indian women aren't discriminated against in law, any more than the men, they have of course been discriminated against by custom for centuries: we have been very tightly held by our traditions and within the family. It's only recently, for example, that the custom of serving the men, and then eating separately in the kitchen, has begun to go – only in the last few years. That was both symbol and reality, as far as our position in the home went! Not all tradition has to go – the family can be a strong framework; it can provide discipline as well as custom. I've been quite firm with my daughters . . . but I don't believe you should force them, in the way they used to be, to live their lives according to the parents' orders. It's actually becoming very hard for any parent to do that, even if they want to: there's a lot of rebellion as well as economic independence.

'Indian women are looking for absolute equality with their husbands now. Most young girls want nothing but equality with their menfolk. In most cases they marry for love – they've met the man before they've married. Matchmaking, where the parents would look for the husband or the wife, doesn't happen any more: the girls won't have it – they will not allow their parents to find their husbands for them. They meet boys today, and if the parents agree, they get married: and if the parents don't agree, they still get married . . . even marrying outside the Muslim community was a very bold step at first: and it's hurt a lot of parents.

'My daughter has married a Muslim, but my son married a Christian girl – it hasn't bothered me a bit. They got married by Muslim rites, but that was purely for convenience – they couldn't get married by civil law because she is white, and as they actually wanted to go through with a formal ceremony this seemed the simplest way. She's just his wife, my daughter-in-law – I never bother to teach her any of the Muslim ways . . . unless she's interested, I won't bother. We had a little ceremony here in the house for them – of course it's still not legal in terms of the South African law, but it was important to them.

'The government has decided that they want to give the vote to Indians and the coloured community – on separate rolls. We've all been told that we have to register now for this voting for a President's Council. We'll register but we won't vote – what the devil would we be voting for? We still wouldn't have the rights that we want . . . blacks haven't been included: we can't accept a partial instrument. And besides, the next thing you'd see would be our sons sent to the border in the army, to fight – they'd be called up to defend this sick system.'

(At the time of this interview, the government had struggled for more than two years to get all Indian adults to register as voters. The campaign, which included written notification that prosecution would follow if registration did not take place, finally netted 80 per cent of the 400,000 who would have been eligible to vote – but the elections, when they took place, were a fiasco as hardly anyone took part.)

Amanda Kwadi

Amanda Kwadi is a young, militant black woman who has been detained four times for her beliefs. She is engaged to journalist Thamsanga Mkhwanazi, who was sentenced to seven years' imprisonment on Robben Island in 1980 for alleged participation in the freedom struggle. Amanda Kwadi works in Johannesburg but occasionally travels 1000 miles to Cape Town, from where she is allowed to go to the island for a short visit to her fiancé. She combined one such

visit with the celebration of South African Women's Day on
August 9, and spoke afterwards of her view of imperialism
and feminism.

'The idea of feminism goes hand in hand with capitalism and
imperialism, something which the Women's Federation in
South Africa denounces. Maybe, as time goes on, there'll be
clarification, but at the moment when we get deep into
feminism it goes so much against African tradition that it's
totally out. We're in the middle of a liberation struggle, but
women's liberation is not necessary at this stage. We are far
more concerned about total liberation; and automatically,
our own liberation will follow. Most of the factors that make
men more dominant arise out of social and political problems
– and we plan to resolve those!

'We have a triple discrimination – we earn less in industry,
in domestic service, in agriculture. We're discriminated
against in law; yes, black women do suffer more than black
men – they're only kept down as blacks and workers. But at
this stage we must struggle for political liberation; probably
afterwards, maybe, some organisation will sit together and
say, OK, now lets talk about women's rights.

'But generally, according to my tradition, I still believe
that a man will remain the head of the family – I'd like that,
with me contributing. We'll sit around and discuss, give
suggestions and opinions. But I wouldn't like to dominate my
man, as an African woman. So-called equality in America: in
fact American women dominate American men, as one big
generalisation – I really believe they've gone about things
the wrong way. I'm engaged . . . we do try and consult each
other before making decisions, although that's sometimes a
bit difficult at present. But, as a man, there are some things
where he must take the decisions, especially in the field of
finance. It does depend to some extent on whether he's a
responsible man.

'I do support equal pay for equal work . . . my parents were
migrant labourers, and they were grateful to earn at all, let
alone the same amount. That didn't exist in those days and
certainly women weren't struggling for it then. I was left at
home with my grandmother in the countryside near Pretoria

because my mother was a domestic worker – my father could only visit her occasionally at nights: he couldn't stay, and there was certainly no room for me. Besides, I couldn't have had any schooling in the white area. So we usually came there during the school holidays – we had to hide, you know! This was in Yeoville, in Johannesburg: we were in special servants' rooms at the top of the flat building, and the police would raid to make sure there were no "illegals" in the building.

'My father was a junior clerk . . . actually we were luckier than most: because we were only about 55 miles from Johannesburg they used to try and visit us perhaps once a month – I have many friends who grew up so far away from their parents they were fortunate to see them once a year, if then. My grandparents were farm labourers: they were paid by being given food. . . . I used to worry and try and understand what was going on. It was when I was in Form 4 at high school, in 1967, that I became aware of the detentions, what was happening to people like Nelson Mandela: I used to read the papers and be concerned to find out why all these people are being detained, why they are in prison – and whether there was a connection with the way my mother and father, and my grandparents, had to work. . . .

'I think black women today are increasingly militant in defence of their rights – but they do see it as part of the liberation of everybody. And as far as the men are concerned we really do work within our own traditions – and for the time that definitely means they must remain as the head of the household.'

Sheena Duncan

'I'm the national president of the Black Sash and director of the Johannesburg Advice Office. I've been involved with the work here since I came back from Zimbabwe in 1963.

'One could do this work from purely selfish, self-interest reasons, because I feel very strongly that the direction South

Africa is going in is disastrous for the whites; much more
than for the black population; so one could just explain it on
that level – a rational reason why people get involved in this
kind of work.

'On a more personal level, I suppose, there's the influence of
my mother: she started the Black Sash, but even before that
she was involved in politics. Therefore all kinds of things –
like conversation at home when I was a child – tended to
range around subjects of public interest. Those were the days
when we had a domestic staff of five people in the house . . .
but my introduction to things being wrong really came from
the headmistress of my school, Ella Lemaitre. She was a
personal friend of Trevor Huddleston and of Alan Paton, so
that some of my very earliest memories of becoming aware
arose from visits to places like Diepkloof Reformatory, which
Paton was running, and having Father Huddleston coming to
talk at school and knowing what kind of work his Community
of the Resurrection was doing in those days.

'They're the kind of churchmen who have intelligently
used their compassion and their knowledge of what goes on in
a wider poltical context. I'm a religous person – that's the real
reason I'm so heavily committed: it's because of my own
Christian understanding, particularly if you are so
privileged as to be born into circumstances where you have
the joy of education, the joy of having books around. All those
privileges that in world terms only a very few have. Only a
few of us enjoy the kind of chances that I have had, without
belonging to a very wealthy family.

'Today, although we do this practical work to try and help
Africans get their rights to stay in the towns and cities, the
Black Sash is also working on things like the franchise which
would enable many more to enjoy similar privileges. We
stand for a universal adult franchise – we are constantly
aware that all kinds of things we're dealing with in this office
wouldn't happen if we had a democracy in this country. The
franchise is the basic issue to all the rest we do.

'Black women have an even heavier burden to bear in this
country, without the vote, than men. We have just been
talking about somebody this morning who is a very old lady,
the wife of a black catechist in Kwazulu whose husband died

quite recently. They never had any children of their own, but they adopted quite a large number: but with only one of them did they go through all the legal processes – he is her only legal son and now, with her husband's death, he is her guardian. She can do nothing whatsoever unless he as her guardian agrees she should be emancipated. There are problems, because he left home long ago and never came near his old parents; now he's reappeared on the scene and the anxiety is that he won't allow this emancipation.

'Now that kind of added oppression of black women, under tribal law and even under civil law in Natal, can affect their lives very profoundly. But it's even more than that – there are a whole lot of things where women are particularly acted against because they bear children – the government's reasons for influx control is to restrain the number of blacks in white areas, so-called. The woman suffer particularly because they bear the children – and if they're born in an urban area they have rights there. So the law on influx control is much more severe for black women than for black men, in practice, and their chances, if they're in rural areas, of ever getting contracts of employment in the white areas are remote.

'They're certainly not allowed to come to town. The discrimination against them is part of population control . . . the whole South African structure discriminates against all women – but white women have more rights than black men, so it's a funny kind of uneven kind of thing. The whole of our society tends to be very Calvinist to women; it's only in the last couple of years that we're getting non-discriminatory legislation about men and women in employment, wage determination and that kind of thing. Black women have the added disadvantage that if you are a black family with very limited means, you tend to expend more of those means on educating your sons than on educating your daughters. For a young woman to get to university is quite something because her brothers will have taken the lion's share of what the family has decided to spend. So there are a million different effects arising from this relative inequality.

'But they're not feminists . . . a woman said to me that the oppression of black people had so emasculated black men that

she didn't feel any desire or even right to put any further
pressure on her husband because it could only further debase
his perception of himself. She saw the greater oppression as
the oppression of the whole people; and there is also a very
real sense in which women are going to find, when liberation
is won, that their liberation has also been part of that process.

'In the South African Council of Churches we find, as we go
about the country with our work, that women are often the
strongest members of a local community, so that most of my
work in the Council lies in teaching women's groups. You do
find that the people involved at the grass roots in the rural
areas tend to be women. It is usually the women who say,
"We've got to organise; we've got to do something about this."
In town you find it's the women who take the whole
responsibility for their families, over and over again. The
man is defeated by the circumstances of his life, so often. . . .

'There's a sort of power of endurance in women . . . their
sense of close responsibility for their children doesn't appear
to be so easily destroyed by the dreadful social conditions. So
often with Soweto families, the man draws his pay packet on
a Friday, drinks most of it on his way home; spends the
weekend, if he is at home, in a drunken stupor that isolates
him from his family.

'It's one of the reasons why, in '76 in the students' revolt,
one of their targets was the beer halls and the liquor outlets.
It crops up over and over again, with youngsters pouring
liquor on to the street . . . the drinking is an escape from
reality, from the pressures of the responsibility for the
children; and women can't escape from that so easily. And
they end up, so often, carrying the whole burden. I believe
this to be true of rural areas as well, where a man comes to
town and works; he's separated from his family and the ties
can get very thin as far as he's concerned. The wife has the
responsibility for rearing the children because he can come
home only once a year; and sometimes he even stops doing
that in the end . . . the family is broken.

'I'm a pacifist myself by conviction . . . therefore I would
never see a solution to the hideous things that go on here in
the taking up of arms. It's hard to ask a white woman about
liberation, because when you analyse what your role is, it

isn't a very glamorous or exciting or anything else kind of role, because the kind of action that white people can take, in civil disobedience for example, is essentially the demonstrative protest, it's not the kind of action that people themselves can take that will change things quite dramatically. It's always got to be, as Gandhi showed, people making some kind of public demonstation – it's the very basis of our Black Sash protest work.

'What our other work does – helping a few people to their minimal rights of staying in an urban area, for example – is that it also helps us understand how the structure works, how the pass laws operate; we then seek every chance to transfer that knowledge to the black community. They've got the vast numbers and the determination, but we can help with this material.'

At typical Black Sash demonstrations the women stand silently, wearing the black sash of mourning, in protest against forced removals, bannings of trade unionists and political figures, detentions without trial. The women stand at a distance from each other because political gatherings in the open air are illegal; they also do indoor vigils. It is an all-woman organisation with one limitation: it is open only to whites.

Winnie Mandela

Winnie Mandela was a social worker when she married African National Congress leader Nelson Mandela in 1958. In twenty-six years of marriage, they have had only two years together. Before he was finally arrested and sentenced to life imprisonment, Nelson Mandela worked underground, continuing the work of the banned ANC. Ms Mandela has been repeatedly subject to detention, house arrest, restriction and imprisonment, as a result of which she initially lost her job as a social worker and subsequently was prohibited from doing any writing. She was detained under the Terrorism Act

in May 1969 and held sleepless for five days and nights while
being interrogated by the security police. During the interrogation she suffered from dizziness, swollen hands and feet,
she had difficulty in breathing and she began to tremble. By
the time she was acquitted she had spent 491 days in solitary
confinement.

Since then she has been repeatedly arrested and charged
with breaking one banning order or another: talking to more
than one person at a time, having her sister visit her at home
when she was ill, talking to a banned person. Convictions,
appeals, acquittals, suspended sentences and short imprison-
ments have followed, and except for a short period of freedom
from September 1975 until August 1976, she has been continually prevented from doing the political campaigning to
which she is dedicated. In 1976, when Soweto students began
their protest against teaching in Afrikaans, when children
and teenagers were shot down by the police, she became a
representative of parents and residents through the Black
Parents' Association: 'We know what we want – our aspirations are dear to us. We are not *asking* for majority rule; it is
our right, we shall have it at any cost.' She was again
arrested, released after five months and banned – this time it
meant she had to stay in the Soweto house at all times and
she could only speak to one person at a time. She describes
detention:

'Detention means that midnight knock when all about you is
quiet. It means those blinding torches shone simultaneously
through every window of your house before the door is kicked
open . . . it means your seizure at dawn, dragged away from
little children screaming and clinging to your skirt,
imploring the man dragging mummy to leave her alone . . . it
means, as it was for me, being held in a single cell with the
light burning twenty-four hours so that I lost track of time
and was unable to tell whether it was day or night. Every
single moment of your life is strictly regulated and
supervised. Complete isolation from the outside world, no
privacy, no visitor, lawyer or minister. It means no one to talk
to each twenty-four hours, no knowledge of how long you will
be imprisoned and why you are imprisoned, getting medical

attention from the doctor only when you are seriously ill . . .
the emptiness of those hours of solitude is unbearable. Your
company is your solitude, your blanket, your mat, your
sanitary bucket, your mug and yourself. All this is in
preparation for the inevitable hell – interrogation. It is
meant to crush your individuality completely, to change you
into a docile being from whom no resistance can arise, to
terrorise you, to intimidate you into silence.'

And her political views today:

'The white man has now reduced the struggle virtually to
black versus white – this is the situation that has been
created for us; we have no choice. They have separated us
completely from them and driven us into a corner where you
can only fight in the context of blackness.

'You can only hit back as a black because you are virtually
isolated – we are told to live in our own areas – you are
isolated in jobs, in almost everything. So life has been
reduced to black versus white and that is the context of the
struggle as a whole.

'Up to 1969, before I was – before then I had just been in and
out of prisons but then I was in solitary confinement for
seventeen months – it's hardly anything to talk about, people
have lost their lives in solitary confinement – it is then that I
really felt made. It is such a hard test of your ideals, and at
the same time it teaches you so much of what you stand for –
your own values.

'Perhaps up to that stage I had not realised the gravity of
our struggle and up to that stage, as a mother and as a black
woman I wouldn't have known what my reaction would be if I
found myself in a violent situation: would I actually take a
gun? And shoot in defence of what I believed in? That was
before I went in for solitary confinement.

'But from that experience I know what I can do in defence of
this my country, in defence of what I believe to be a just
society. I believe that now."

In 1977 Winnie Mandela was again banished – this time
from Soweto to house no. 802 in the black area outside the

town of Brandfort in the Orange Free State, hundreds of miles from Johannesburg. With characteristic energy, she started a children's clinic with local friends. Gradually, she has been able to visit her husband more frequently – 'It has been a very slow change and a painful process . . . it is less than two years now, that I have been able to touch him and to hold him . . .' In 1985, when Nelson Mandela, who had been moved from the penal colony at Robben Island to Pollsmoor gaol, went into a Cape Town hospital for a prostate operation, Mrs Mandela was able to see him every day for the first time in twenty-five years.

Her own personal struggle against apartheid's decrees continues unabated. The home outside Brandfort was burnt down while she was on a medical visit to Johannesburg (in her judgement the work of right-wing extremists), and she decided to break the banishment order and remain in Soweto. For the last five months of 1985 she moved about freely; it was not until she appeared unexpectedly at a funeral near Pretoria that had turned into a mass political rally, that the police arrested and charged her. In 1986 she won her case against the police and returned to Soweto.

Winnie Mandela is emerging now as a powerful and important symbol in the freedom struggle in her own right. She told me 'When you get married in apartheid South Africa, when you get married in a society that is so sick that every aspect of your life is political, you hardly ever marry the man. There are no romantic dreams – when you marry you marry the cause of your people. I knew the road would be uphill: I knew history would determine my private life'. She was referring to Nelson when she said that, but it applies as much now to her own political role.

Here she talks of detention and her belief about the future:

'I was one of the first victims under the Terrorist Act: we were a test case when we were held in solitary confinement for 18 months. Conditions were extremely bad; we were held incommunicado. There is nothing as soul-destroying, as dehumanising and as beastly as that form of harassment. The purpose is to shatter your soul, to so demoralise you –

they hope – that you actually change your views. What they do forget is that you can detain the physical being, but your ideals can never be detained: if anything, you simply solidify them.

'The act of detention is an act of violence. You serve a sentence for a crime for which you have not been tried. Thousands of people – black and white; men, women and children – die in that detention every year.

'Our people are unarmed. No matter how brave one can be, it's not possible to retaliate – for the mass of the people – against this heavily armed government. The people of this land, on all occasions, have reacted and responded to the violence of the government. Even the African National Congress had to arrive at the decision to respond to the violence and terror of the system with grave difficulties.

'People's anger has been bottled up generation after generation. The protests have continued over many years against our living conditions, against apartheid as an act of violence; against the partitioning of our land, against forced removals, against the whole concept of separate development.

'No solution in this land will ever be effective if it is exclusive of the majority here – that is all we have been saying. A future South Africa, which we will realise at whatever cost, is a South Africa where each one of us, each person, has a right to cast his vote, each one of us has a right to the wealth of this land – we live in a country which is rich enough to hold all its inhabitants.

'We will determine what sort of government we want – it is our own business.'

EPILOGUE

By June, 1986 South Africa's president, P.W. Botha, had promised more reforms. The hated pass laws had been lifted at last – only to be replaced by the control of movement of black people about the country through new identity documents, coupled with the need to have a home in the urban area where they sought work. The nationalist government appears to be on the run – the more violent the police and the army daily become, the less they are in control; and violence breeds fresh violence daily.

But there has been no indication from Botha, or any of his ministers, of a move towards the one necessity that would begin to bring to an end unrest and misery and death for twenty-six million black people in South Africa: the beginning of discussion and negotiation for a fully democratic State for all South Africans, whatever the colour of their skins. There are suggestions for new provincial councils, and for a black 'advisory' council – derisory and meaningless changes in a country where too many have lived under virtual slavery for too long.

In the quickening twilight of white supremacist South Africa, lit today more by gunfire than its endless sunshine, there are some moments that clarify this struggle for human dignity; and it is not a battle of black against white. In May, yet another funeral of black men and women who had been shot by the police was due to take place in the black township of Alexandra near Johannesburg. More than three hundred whites defied a police cordon and tear gas to go to that funeral. They were greeted with handshakes and hugs, with kisses and tears. There was love that day in Johannesburg, rather than hatred. And the tide of change moves, now, inexorably forward.

P A N D O R A   P R E S S

an imprint of Routledge and Kegan Paul

For further information about Pandora Press books, please write to the Mailing List Dept at Pandora Press, 39 Store Street, London WC1E 7DD; or in the USA at 9, Park Street, Boston, Mass. 02108; or in Australia at 6th Floor, 464 St. Kilda Road, Melbourne, Victoria 3004, Australia.

Some Pandora titles you may enjoy:

WOMEN'S HISTORY IN SHORT STORIES

the companion volume to Old Maids

DARING TO DREAM

Utopian stories by United States women: 1836-1919

Compiled, edited and introduced by Carol Farley Kessler

Carol Farley Kessler has unearthed an extraordinary assortment of visionary writing, writings which encapsulate all the yearnings of a vanished generation for a future which has still to be made. Some women write with irony, describing journeys through time and space to parallel but inverted worlds where sober-suited women run commerce and affairs of state while men either prink and preen in beribboned breeches, or are weakened by the burden of unending housework. Other writers lay out complicated blueprints for a non-sexist society. One woman dreams, touchingly, of a fantastic future where men get up in the night to comfort crying children. The stories demonstrate that even in the early nineteenth century women were arguing that male and female 'character traits' were the product of their roles, not of their biology; and they make apparent the hidden roots of the discontent, longing and anger which was later to erupt in the great movements of women for change.

0-86358-013-0 Fiction/Social History 256pp 198 × 129 mm paperback

DISCOVERING WOMEN'S HISTORY

a practical manual .

Deirdre Beddoe

Rainy Sunday afternoons, long winter evenings: why not set yourself a research project, either on your own or in a group or classroom? This is the message from Deirdre Beddoe, an historian who tears away the mystique of her own profession in this step-by-step guide to researching the lives of ordinary women in Britain from 1800 to 1945. *Discovering Women's History* tells you how to get started on the detective trail of history and how to stalk your quarry through attics and art galleries, museums and old newspapers, church archives and the Public Records Office – and how to publish your findings once you have completed your project.

'an invaluable and fascinating guide to the raw material for anyone approaching this unexplored territory' *The Sunday Times*

'Thrilling and rewarding and jolly good fun' *South Wales Argus*

0-86358-008-4 Hobbies/Social History 232pp 198 × 129 mm illustrated

ALL THE BRAVE PROMISES

Memories of Aircraftwomen 2nd Class 2146291

Mary Lee Settle

Mary Lee Settle was a young American woman living a comfortable life in Washington D.C. when the Second World War broke out. In 1942 she boarded a train, carrying 'a last bottle of champagne and an armful of roses', and left for England to join the WAAF. She witnessed the horror of war – the bombing raids, the planes lost in fog, the children evacuated, a blacked-out Britain of austerity and strain. She also witnessed the women, her fellow recruits, as they struggled to adapt to their new identities and new lives at the bottom of the uniformed pile. Dedicated 'to the wartime other ranks of the Women's Auxiliary Air Force – below the rank of Sergeant', this rare book captures women's wartime experience; a remarkable and important story by one of America's prizewinning novelists.

'One of the most moving accounts of war experience ever encountered' *Library Journal*

0-86358-033-5 General/Autobiography 160pp 198 × 129 mm paperback

not for sale in the U.S.A. or Canada

MY COUNTRY IS THE WHOLE WORLD

an anthology of women's work on peace and war

Cambridge Women's Peace Collective (eds.)

Women's struggle for peace is no recent phenomenon. In this book, the work of women for peace from 600 BC to the present is documented in a unique collection of extracts from songs, poems, diaries, letters, petitions, pictures, photographs and pamphlets through the ages. A book to give as a gift, to read aloud from, to research from, to teach from, *My Country is the Whole World* is both a resource and an inspiration for all who work for peace today.

'an historic document . . . readers will be amazed at the extent of the collection' *Labour Herald*

'a beautifully presented and illustrated book which makes for accessible and enlightening reading' *Morning Star*

0-86358-004-1 Social Questions/History 306pp A5 illustrated throughout paperback